Provincial Gazetteer of Assam

Provincial Gazetteer of Assam

Compiled by Authority

GYAN

ISBN : 978-81-212-0635-8

Published, 2018

Published by

Gyan Publishing House
5, Ansari Road
Daryaganj, New Delhi-110002
Phone: 011-47034999, 9811692060
www.gyanbooks.com
E-mail: books@gyanbooks.com

Printed at: G. Print Process, Delhi.

CONTENTS.

PHYSICAL ASPECTS.

HISTORY.

POPULATION.

AGRICULTURE.

RENTS, WAGES, AND PRICES.

FORESTS.

MINES AND MINERALS.

ARTS AND MANUFACTURES.

COMMERCE AND TRADE.

MEANS OF COMMUNICATION.

GOVERNMENT AND ADMINISTRATIVE DIVISIONS.

LEGISLATION AND JUSTICE.

FINANCE.

LAND REVENUE.

MISCELLANEOUS REVENUE.

LOCAL AND MUNICIPAL.

PUBLIC WORKS.

POLICE AND JAILS.

EDUCATION.

MEDICAL.

TABLES.

MINOR NOTICES.

HILLS.

RIVERS.

PROVINCIAL GAZETTEER

OF

ASSAM.

[Since the following article was written the small province of Assam has ceased to exist as a separate unit, and has been amalgamated with 15 districts of Northern and Eastern Bengal to form the larger province of Eastern Bengal and Assam, which is ruled by a Lieutenant-Governor assisted by a Council. The account of the general administrative staff, the various departments, and the system of legislation is thus obsolete and the arrangements which are now in force will be found described in the article on Eastern Bengal and Assam. The remainder of the article still affords a generally correct account of that portion of the new province which was once known as Assam.]

PHYSICAL ASPECTS.

Boundaries and Area.

ASSAM.—The Province of Assam, which lies on the north-eastern border of Bengal, and is one of the frontier Provinces of the Indian Empire, is situated between 22° 19′ and 28° 18′ N. and 89° 42′ and 97° 12′ E. It is bounded on the north by the eastern section of the great Himālayan range, the frontier tribes from west to east being successively the Bhotiās of Bhutān, the Bhotiās of Towang,—a province subject to Lhāsa,—Akās, Daflās, Miris, Abors, and Mishmis; on the north-east by the Mishmi Hills, which sweep round the head of the Brahmaputra Valley, on the east by the mountains which are inhabited by Khamtis, Singphos, and various Nāgā tribes; and by the Burmese frontier, where it marches with that of the Manipur State; on the south by the Chin Hills, the Chittagong Hill Tracts, and the State of Hill Tippera; and on the west by the districts of Tippera, Mymensingh, and Rangpur, the State of Cooch Behār, and Jalpaigurī District. The total area of the Province, including the Native State of Manipur (8,456 square miles), is 61,682 square miles.

Origin of name.

The name "Assam" is, according to some, derived from the Sanskrit "Asama," which means peerless or unequalled. It has been suggested that this title was applied to the Shan invaders, who are now called Ahoms, and transferred from them to the country that they conquered. This derivation is, however, open to the serious objection that in Assamese *s* is softened into *h*, as in the name of the tribe; and there is no apparent reason why it should have been retained in the name of the country. It is doubtful also whether either the Ahoms themselves, or the tribes they found in occupation of the country, would use a Sanskrit term to denote the dominant race.

Natural divisions.

The Province falls into three natural divisions; the valley of the Surmā or Barāk, the valley of the Brahmaputra, and the intervening range of hills. The Native State of Manipur, which lies east of Cāchār, is under the control of the Local Administration, and the hills to the south of that District inhabited by the Lushais have recently been brought under British rule.

The Surma Valley.

The Surmā Valley is a flat plain about 125 miles long by 60 wide, shut in on three sides by ranges of hills. The river from which the Valley takes its name rises on the southern slopes of the mountain ranges on the borders of the Nāgā Hills District, and flows south through the Manipur hills. At Tipaimukh, it turns sharply to the north and takes a tortuous course, with a generally westward direction, through the Cāchār District. On the western boundary of Cāchār it divides into two branches, the northern of which is known as the SURMA, and flows near the Khāsi Hills past Sylhet and Chhātak, till it turns south at Sunāmganj. The southern branch, called at first the Kusiyārā, again divides into two streams, known as the Barāk and the Bibiyānā, or Kālni, but both branches rejoin the Surmā on the western boundary of the Province. The chief tributaries of the river on the north, after it enters British territory, are the JIRI and JATINGA from the North Cāchār hills, and the BOGAPANI and JADUKATA from the Khāsi and Jaintiā Hills. On the south it receives from the Lushai Hills the SONAI, the DHALESWARI with its second channel, the Kātākhāl, and the SINGLA, and the LANGAI MANU, and KHOWAI from Hill Tippera.

The western end of the valley lies very low, and at Sylhet the low-water level of the Surmā is only 22·7 feet above the sea. The banks of the rivers are raised by deposits of silt above the level of the surrounding country, and are lined with villages, which in the rainy season appear to be standing in a huge lake. Further east the country rises, and fields covered with *sail* (transplanted winter rice) take the place of swamps, in which only the longest-stemmed varieties of paddy can be grown; but even here there are numerous depressions, or *haors* as they are called, in the lowest parts of which water remains during the dry season, and which can only be used for grazing or the growth of winter crops. In western Sylhet the houses of the villagers are crowded together, gardens and fruit trees are scarce, and the scenery at all seasons of the year is tame and uninteresting. Cāchār and the eastern portion of Sylhet have, on the other hand, much to please the eye. Blue hills bound the view on almost every side, the villages are buried in groves of slender palms, feathery bamboos, and broad-leaved plantains, and even in the dry season the country looks fresh and green. The level of the plain is broken up by low ranges and isolated hills, and here and there beds of reeds and marshes lend variety to the scene. Little or no forest exists in Sylhet, but there are extensive reserves in the south and east of the Cāchār District.

The Brahmaputra Valley.

The Brahmaputra Valley is an alluvial plain about 450 miles in length, with an average breadth of about 50 miles, shut in, like the Surmā Valley, by hills on every side except the west. In its lower portion it lies almost east and west, but in its upper half it trends somewhat towards the north-east. The BRAHMAPUTRA flows through the centre of this plain, and receives in its course the drainage of the Himālayas on the north, and the Assam Range on the south. The principal tributaries on the north bank are the DIBANG, DIHANG, SUBANSIRI, BHARELI, DHANSIRI, BARNADI, MANAS, with its tributary the AI, the CHAMPAMATI, SARALBHANGA and SANKOSH; on the south, the greater affluents are the Noa and the Buri DIHINGS, the DISANG, DIKHO, JHANZI, and DHANSIRI. A short distance below the junction with the Dhansiri a considerable body of water separates itself from the Brahmaputra, and, under the name of the KALANG, flows with a tortuous course through the Nowgong District, rejoining the main stream about ten miles above Gauhati. The KALANG receives the KAPILI, which brings to it a large part of the drainage of the Mīkīr, the North Cāchār, and the Jaintiā Hills, and the DIGRU from the Khāsi Hills. Below Gauhāti the most considerable affluents on the south bank are the KULSI and JINJIRAM.

The valley, as a whole, is a level plain of fairly uniform breadth, except in the centre, where the Mīkīr Hills project from the main mass of the Assam Range, almost up to the southern bank of the Brahmaputra. Between Tezpur and Dhubri there are outcrops of gneissic rock above the alluvium, even on the north bank of the river, and the central portion of the Goālpāra District is much broken up by ranges of low hills, but elsewhere there is little to interrupt the even level of the plain.

The Brahmaputra, through the greater part of its course, is bounded on either side by stretches of marsh land covered with thick grass jungle, interspersed here and there with patches of mustard and summer rice. Further inland the level rises, and there is a belt, usually of considerable breadth, of permanent cultivation. The plain is covered with rice fields and dotted over with clumps of bamboos, palms, and fruit trees, in which are buried the houses of the cultivators. In most parts of the valley this belt supports a fairly dense population, but nearer the hills cultivation again falls off, and grassy plains and forests stretch to their feet. Even here, however, rice is grown on fields irrigated from the hill streams, and European enterprise has in many places felled the forests and opened perous tea gardens. Little of this is seen by the traveller on river steamer, and he is liable to receive the impression that m is a wilderness of impenetrable jungle, the home of nothing wild beasts. This view is but partially correct. There are large areas of waste land, swamps, and forests, and hills; but in of the valley the population is beginning to press upon soil, and little good land remains available for settlement. places in the Brahmaputra Valley would not appeal to a of the picturesque. On a clear day the view both to the and south is bounded by hills, while behind the lower ranges e Himālayas snowy peaks glisten in the sun. The rice fields are spersed with groves of feathery bamboos, on every side are pools, s, and woods, and in the wilder parts nature is seen freed the restraining hand of man. The slopes of the lower hills are ed with forest, and the rivers that debouch upon the plain through gorges of exceptional beauty.

The range of mountains which separates these two valleys cts at right angles from the Burmese system, and lies almost east and west. At its western end it attains a height of more 4,600 feet in the peak of Nokrek, above the station of Turā. hills are here broken up into sharply-serrated ridges and deep ys, all alike covered with forest. Further east, in the Shillong they reach a height of 6,450 feet, but this is only the highest in a table-land hardly any part of which falls much below rel of 6,000 feet. The denser forest growth has here disared, and there are wide stretches of rolling down, dotted with ps of oak and pine. On their southern face the hills rise like vel wall abruptly from the plain, with occasionally a deep e, which the rivers, fed by the heavy rainfall of that region, cut through the plateau. Towards the Jaintiā and North ār hills the level falls, but the BARAIL range, which commences he south-east margin of the Khāsi-Jaintiā plateau, rises by en leaps to a considerable height, and among the hills border- the Jātingā valley summits of from 5,000 to 6,000 feet found. Further east, the highest point in the province is ed in JAPVO, on the border of the Nāgā Hills District. The here are all of the serrated type, and their sides are clothed with t or, on the sites of fallowing *jhūms*,* with dense bamboo or grass le. The Lushai Hills, which divide Burma from Assam, run ght angles to the Assam Range. They are for the most part red with bamboo jungle and rank undergrowth, but in the rn portion open grass-covered slopes are found, with groves of and pine, interspersed with rhododendron. The Manipur State ists of a fertile valley, covering an area of about 650 square s, surrounded by ranges of hills.

---

jhum is a piece of land which has been cleared and cultivated for two or three s and then allowed a rest for several years, see page 43.

Lakes and islands.

Numerous swamps and *jhils* in both valleys, and during the rains the western portion of Sylhet lies under water; but in British territory there are no lakes of any considerable importance during the dry season. In Manipur the LOKTAK, a sheet of water covering about 27 square miles, lies to the south of Imphal, the capital town. The only island of any size is the MAJULI, a tract of land covering 485 square miles in the Sibsāgar District, which is surrounded by the waters of the Brahmaputra and the Subansiri.

Geology.*

The Surmā Valley is an alluvial tract, in which the process of deltaic formation has not proceeded so rapidly as in the rest of the Gangetic plain. Disastrous floods were more common at the end of the 18th century than they are at the present day, and it seems possible that the general level of the district may have been appreciably raised within the last hundred years, by the silting up of depressions and the sediment deposited by the rivers in their annual inundations. Low ranges of hills, which for the most part consist of upper tertiary sandstones, project into the Valley from the south, and its surface is dotted with isolated hills called *tilas*, from 50 to 200 feet high, composed of layers of sand, clay, and gravel, often highly indurated with ferruginous cement. In the centre of the Assam Valley the soil consists of a light layer of clay superimposed upon beds of sand. Further back from the Brahmaputra the alluvium is more consolidated, and here and there are to be found the remains of an older alluvium of a closer and heavier texture, which corresponds to the high land of the Gangetic plain. Outliers of gneissic rock from the Assam Range are common between Goālpāra and Gauhāti, and are found as far east as Tezpur.

The basis of the Assam Range is a gneissic rock. At its western end sandstones and conglomerates, which are referable to the cretaceous system, are superimposed upon the gneiss, and are themselves overlaid by limestone and sandstone of the nummulitic age. Further eastwards what is known as the Shillong plateau rises steeply from the Surmā Valley, but on its northern face falls away in a series of low hills towards the Brahmaputra. The gneiss is here succeeded by the Shillong or transition series, which consists of quartzites, conglomerates, phyllites, and schists, through which appear granite and dioritic rocks. Upon this series have been superimposed sandstones and conglomerates of the cretaceous age, which contain occasional coal seams, and which are in their turn overlaid by beds of the nummulitic or lower tertiary period, consisting of limestone and sandstone with interstratified shales and coal deposits. Along the southern edge of the plateau in the neighbourhood of Cherrapunji, a group of bedded basaltic rocks, known as the Sylhet trap, has been forced up between the cretaceous and the older formations. The Mymensingh border is

* This section has been compiled from notes furnished by Mr. P. N. Bose, of the Geological Survey of India, and from an account of Assam by Sir Charles Lyall, published in the General Administration Report of the Province for 1882-1883.

fringed by low ranges of hills of upper tertiary formation, and though this series has been almost entirely removed by denudation below the southern scarp of the Khāsi Hills, they appear again in force east of Jaintiāpur, and their soft, massive, greenish sandstones rise rapidly from this point into the Barail range. This range appears to have thrust the nummulitic and older formations in a north-easterly direction, but west of Cāchār itself curves to the north-east, and finally merges into the Burmese mountain system, of which it forms a part. Little is known of the eastern extremity of the Assam Range, but it appears that the upper tertiary sandstones are succeeded by a series of hard sandstones, slates, and shales with quartzose beds, while still further east serpentine dykes, identical in composition with those of Burma, run north and south. Upper tertiary rocks are believed to constitute the Pātkai range, and are found again capping the hills which look down upon the Chindwin Valley, but between these two points there intervenes a belt of pretertiary beds about 100 miles in width. The hills containing the coal measures of Sibsāgar and Lakhimpur consist of an enormous thickness of sandstones, the upper series of which are topped by conglomerates and clay. The Himālayas north of the Brahmaputra have never been properly explored, but there is reason to suppose that they are composed of great thicknesses of soft massive sandstones, of tertiary age and freshwater origin. The economic aspect of the geology of the Province is referred to in the section on mines and minerals.

Botany. The uncultivated portions of the Assam Valley are usually covered with forest, or with grass and reeds, which are sometimes nearly twenty feet in height. The three commonest varieties are *ikra* (*Saccharum arundinaceum*), *nal* (*Phragmites Roxburghii*) and *khagari* (*Saccharum spontaneum*). At the western end the prevalent tree is *sāl* (*Shorea robusta*), but further east the forests are evergreen, the chief constituents being species of *Amoora*, *Michelia*, *Magnolia*, *Stereospermum*, *Quercus*, *Castanopsis*, *Ficus*, and *Mesua*. Various kinds of palms, cane, tree ferns, bamboos, and plantain trees are common. The vegetation of Sylhet and Cāchār does not differ materially from that of eastern Bengal. There is comparatively little forest, but in the swampy parts numerous species of reeds and aquatic plants are found. The greater part of the Assam Range is covered with dense tree forest or bamboo jungle, but the Khāsi plateau is a fine succession of rolling downs dotted with groves of oak and pine. The flora of this tract is extremely rich, and upwards of 2,000 flowering plants were collected by Dr. Hooker within 10 miles of Cherrapunji, while various kinds of orchids and balsams, rhododendrons, azaleas, and wild roses are found on every side. The Nāgā and Manipur Hills have a flora in many respects similar to that of the Khāsi Hills, but in addition possess a distinct Sikkim element, while the Lushai Hills are botanically part of the Burmese system.

The most noteworthy wild animals are elephants, rhinoceros, tigers, leopards, bears, wild dogs, wild pig, deer, buffaloes, and mithan (*Bos gaurus*). The smaller mithan (*Bos frontalis*) has been domesticated by the wild tribes, and it is doubtful whether it is now found in Assam in a wild state. Rhinoceros are of three kinds, the large variety (*unicornis*), which lives in the swamps that fringe the Brahmaputra, the smaller variety (*sondaicus*), which is occasionally met with in the same locality, and the small two-horned rhinoceros (*Sumatrensis*), which is now and again seen in the hills south of the Surmā Valley, though its ordinary habitat is Sumatra, Borneo and the Malay Peninsula. The ordinary varieties of deer found in the Province are the *sāmbhar* (*Cervus unicolor*), the *bara singha* or swamp deer (*Cervus duvaucelli*), the hog deer (*Cervus porcinus*), and the barking deer (*cervalus muntjac*). Goat-antelopes (*Nemorhaedus Sumatrensis*) are occasionally met with on the higher hills, but are scarce and shy. Elephants are found in considerable numbers in the Assam Valley and in the lower slopes of the Assam Range. They are also occasionally hunted with success in south Cāchār and in south-eastern Sylhet. Extensive operations have been undertaken by the Government Khedah department, and *mahāls*, or the right of hunting within certain areas not reserved for that department, are leased by auction sale to the highest bidder, who pays a royalty of Rs. 100 on each animal captured. During the period when the Government kheddas were working in the Gāro Hills about 400 elephants were annually captured in the Province. Small game include florican, partridges, pheasants, pea and jungle fowl, wild geese and duck, snipe, and hares. Excellent mahseer fishing is also obtained in some of the rivers. **Wild animals.**

The climate of Assam is characterised by coolness and extreme humidity, the natural result of the great water surface and extensive forests over which evaporation and condensation go on, and the close proximity of the hill ranges, on which an excessive precipitation takes place. Its most distinguishing feature is the copious rainfall between March and May, at a time when precipitation over northern India is at its minimum. The year is thus roughly divided into two seasons, the cold weather and the rains, the hot weather of the rest of India being completely absent. From the beginning of November till the end of February the climate is cool and extremely pleasant, and at no period of the year is the heat excessive. Table I, appended to this article, shows the mean temperature and diurnal range in January, May, July, and November at Silchar, Sibsāgar, and Dhubri, the only stations in the Province at which observations have been systematically recorded for any considerable period. Except in the height of the rains, the mean temperature is appreciably lower at Sibsāgar than at Dhubri. This is partly due to the heavy fogs, which in the cold weather frequently hang over the upper part of the Brahmaputra Valley till a late hour of the day and prevent the country from being **Climate and temperature** warmed by the rays of the sun. In the Surmā Valley the thermometer in the winter is from five to six degrees higher than in upper Assam, but during the remainder of the year the climate of Sylhet is fairly cool. Cāchār has a higher mean temperature for the year than any other District in the Province. On the Shillong plateau the thermometer seldom rises above 80° in the shade at the hottest season of the year, and ice forms on shallow pools in the winter nights. Fogs occur in the Surmā Valley, but are not as common as in central and upper Assam, where at certain seasons of the year they are a serious impediment to steamer traffic. In the Surmā Valley the prevailing wind is from the south-west, except in the months of April and May, when it has a north-north-east direction. In the Brahmaputra Valley the wind is usually from the north-east. In July and August the wind blows from the south-west in Assam proper and from the south-east in the Goālpāra District.

Rainfall. The total amount of rain that falls in Assam during the year is always abundant, but is sometimes unfavourably distributed. In the Surmā Valley, the average rainfall at Sylhet is 157 inches, and at Silchar 124. To the south of the valley precipitation is less pronounced, but deluges of rain fall on the southern slopes of the Khāsi Hills and pour down into the valley. The average annual rainfall at Cherrapunji is 458 inches, and in 1861, 905 inches are said to have fallen, of which 503 inches were recorded in the months of June and July. Goālpāra and Lakhimpur, at the two ends of the Assam Valley, receive about 115 inches of rain during the year. Kāmrūp, Nowgong, and Darrang are to some extent protected by the high plateaux of the Khāsi Hills, and the rainfall of these Districts ranges from 71 to 77 inches. At Lankā, in the Kapili valley in Nowgong, the average annual fall is less than 43 inches, but a little to the east the level of the hills that separate the Brahmaputra and Surmā Valleys falls, and the rainfall in Sibsāgar rises to 85 inches. The percentage of the absolute range on the average annual fall is 70 in the Surmā and 68 in the Assam Valley. The rainfall in the hill Districts is ample, but at the few stations at which observations have been recorded its character is largely determined by local conditions, and the average rainfall of this region is probably larger than the figures would suggest. Statistics of monthly rainfall are shown in table II.

Storms and floods. Storms often occur in the spring months, generally accompanied by high winds and heavy local rainfall, but seldom take the form of destructive cyclones. Two such, however, visited the country at the foot of the Gāro Hills in 1900, destroying everything in their path, and killing 44 people. The Province has always suffered more from floods than from a failure of the water-supply. The rainfall, which is everywhere heavy, is in places enormous, and the rivers are frequently unable to carry off the torrents of water suddenly precipitated on their catchment areas. In Mughal times the country in the neighbourhood of the upper portion of the Barāk was protected by an embankment, but at the western end of the Surmā Valley it has always been impossible to restrain the torrential floods, and the whole surface of the plain goes under water. In 1781 a sudden rise of the rivers wrought such utter desolation that, in spite of the efforts of Government, nearly one-third of the population died of famine; but, though inundations annually occur, no such calamities have been known of recent years. In the Assam Valley floods were always one of the chief obstacles to the Muhammadan invaders, and the rivers in Sibsāgar, where there was a large Ahom population, were protected by strong embankments. With the disappearance of the native system of compulsory labour, these works were allowed to fall into disrepair, but steps have recently been taken for the restoration of the more important among them. Except in a few places, where the high bank comes down to the water's edge, the floods of the Brahmaputra render a broad belt of land on either side of the river unfit for ordinary cultivation in the rains, and a considerable amount of local damage is sometimes done by the spill water of its tributaries. The earthquake of 1897 in some way affected the drainage channels and levels of the country, and since that date the floods, especially in lower Assam, have been of greater duration and intensity. Large tracts, which used formerly to bear rich crops of mustard, remain too long under water to admit of the seed being sown, and special works were rendered necessary for the protection of GOALPARA and BARPETA, as after the earthquake the towns were found to be below flood level. The condition of Barpetā was subsequently much improved by drainage works in which the people co-operated without payment.

Assam has always been subject to earthquakes. In 1607 A.D. Earthquakes. hills are said to have been rent asunder and swallowed up, and McCosh, writing in 1837, reports that some 20 years before, a village standing on a knoll near Goālpāra completely disappeared, a pool of water appearing in its place. Severe shocks were felt at Silchar in 1869 and 1882, and in 1875 some damage was done to houses in Shillong and Gauhāti. All previous seismic disturbances were, however, completely thrown in the shade by the earthquake of June 12th, 1897, which was the most severe and disastrous of which there is any record in Assam. The station of Shillong was levelled with the ground, and women and children were for several days exposed to drenching rain, with no better shelter than could be obtained from a few tents and tumble-down stables, and sheds without floors or walls. Nearly all masonry buildings in Gauhāti and Sylhet were completely wrecked, and much damage was done in Goālpāra, Nowgong and Darrang. Two Europeans and 1,540 natives lost their lives, the majority of the latter being killed by landslips in the hills and by the falling in of river banks in Sylhet. Roads and bridges were destroyed, and the drainage of the country was seriously affected by the silting up of streams and watercourses. The total cost incurred on special repairs to public works necessitated by the earthquake exceeded 37 lakhs of rupees, but, even with this sum, it was impossible to restore them to their former condition. Of the damage done to private property it is difficult to form an estimate.

HISTORY

Prehistoric movements of the people.

The early history of the Province is very obscure. In the two great river valleys, especially in that of the Surmā, the population contains a certain admixture of Dravidian blood, but, in the main, Assam has drawn its inhabitants from the great hive of the Mongolian race in western China, which in very ancient times threw off a series of swarms that afterwards found their way into the frontier lands of India—some to the west, ascending the San-po or upper course of the Brahmaputra, and so along the northern slopes of the Himālayas; some to the south, down the courses of the Chindwin, Irrawaddy, Salween, Menam, and Mekong rivers, peopling Burma, Siam, and the adjoining countries; and some to the south-west, descending the Brahmaputra to Assam and thence far into Bengal. It is with these last that we are here concerned. Their main line of movement was probably along the banks of the Brahmaputra, and as each swarm was forced in turn to yield to the pressure from behind, it either moved on westwards or turned aside into the hills of the Assam Range.

Legends from Hindu sources.

The first mention of the country which we now call Assam is found in the epics and religious legends of Gangetic India, but it is not yet possible to unravel the slender thread of real fact from the tangled skein of fable, invention, and poetical exaggeration. Aryan priests and warriors undoubtedly found their way thither in very early times, but they were wanting in the historic instinct, and left no trustworthy record behind them. Various places mentioned in the story of Krishna and in the Mahābhārata are now identified with sites in the Province, but many of them are also claimed, probably with better reason, by other parts of India. Among much that is vague or dubious one fact stands out clearly. There is no doubt whatever that the temple of Sakti, Siva's consort, at Kāmākhya near Gauhāti, was famous in very ancient times, and that it was a great centre of the bloody and sensual form of worship inculcated in the Tantras, which probably had its origin there. The Kālikā Purāna and Jogini Tantra preserve the names of several kings, whose titles, Dánava and Asura, betray their aboriginal descent, and who were followed by Naraka, the reputed founder of the ancient and famous city of Prāgjyotishapura, the modern Gauhāti. According to tradition, Naraka ruled from the Karatoyá river to the extreme east of the Brahmaputra valley, and met his death at the hands of Krishna. He was succeeded by his son Bhagadatta, whose name finds frequent mention in the Mahābhārata as the Lord of Prāgjyotisha and the powerful ally of Duryodhana: he had, it is narrated, a great army of Chīnas and Kirátas, but was defeated and slain by Arjuna on the fatal field of Kurukshetra.

Reliable history is first reached in the narrative of the Chinese pilgrim Hiuen Tsiang, who visited the country then known as Kámarūpa, about 640 A.D., and found it occupied by a race with dark yellow complexions, small in stature, and fierce in appearance, but upright and studious. Their king was Kumára Bhāskara Varman,* and they followed the Brāhmanical religion. Hiuen Tsiang's description of the country.

Of the next few centuries our knowledge is very slight, but the gloom is to some extent dispelled by the recent discovery of several inscribed copper-plates,† which appear to have been prepared between the latter part of the tenth and the middle of the twelfth century. The primary object of these inscriptions was to recite the grant of land to Brāhmans, but to us their most interesting part is the preamble wherein some account is given of the Chief by whom each grant was made and of his ancestry. It would seem that soon after Hiuen Tsiang's departure the country fell into the hands of a line of aboriginal chiefs who were subsequently converted to Hinduism. Then followed a dynasty founded by one Pralambha, who killed or banished all the members of the previous ruling family. The sixth in descent from him was Bala Varman, in whose reign the first of the copper-plate documents above referred to was executed. These kings were worshippers of Siva; their capital was at a place called Hárúppesvara, but they still called themselves Lords of Prāgjyotisha. Early in the eleventh century they were succeeded by a fresh line of kings, who, like their predecessors, claimed descent from the mythical Naraka. The third prince of this family was Ratnapála, "the mighty crusher of his enemies, who studded the earth with whitewashed temples and the skies with the smoke of his burnt offerings." He got much wealth from his copper mines (in Bhutān?); and he erected, it is alleged, pillar monuments of his victories, and built a new capital, which became the home of many wealthy merchants, learned men, priests and poets. Some time later the country seems to have been conquered, first by the Sen kings of Bengal, and then by their rivals, the well-known Pāl kings, whose vassal, Tishya Deva, rebelled about 1133 and was defeated by the Pāl general Vaidyadeva, who in his turn seems to have made himself practically independent. The area ruled by these different kings varied greatly from time to time. Sometimes it stretched as far west Copper plate inscriptions of tenth to twelfth centuries.

* Varman is a Kshattriya title, but it is often assumed by aristocratic converts to Hinduism.

† Dr. Hoernle's readings of some of these plates which were obtained by Mr. E. A. Gait and sent to him for decipherment will be found in the Journal of the Asiatic Society of Bengal for 1897.

as the Karatoyá river and, if their panegyrists can be believed, as far south as the sea coast, including within its limits the Surmā Valley, eastern Bengal, and, occasionally, Bhután : at other times, it did not even comprise the whole of what is now known as the Brahmaputra Valley: sometimes again, and perhaps this was the more usual condition, the country was split up into a number of petty principalities each under its own chief. The Surmā Valley, at any rate, was usually independent of the kings of Kāmarūpa. The early history of this tract is even more obscure than that of the Brahmaputra Valley : we know, however, from copper-plate inscriptions that in the first half of the thirteenth century it was ruled by a king named Govinda Deva, and subsequently by his son Isāna Deva, but we possess little information regarding them beyond the fact that they were Hindus.

More recent traditions. According to the traditions of the Mahāpurushias, lower Assam and the adjacent part of Bengal subsequently formed a kingdom called Kāmata, and its ruler at the beginning of the fourteenth century was a prince named Durlabh Nārāyan. In the fifteenth century a line of Khen kings rose to power in the same tract of country. The third and last of this line, Nilāmbar, was overthrown in 1498 by Husain Sháh, the Muhammadan king of Bengal, who, after a long siege, took the capital, Kāmatapur, by a stratagem.

The Koch kings. A few years later Biswa Singh laid the foundation of the Koch kingdom, and, after defeating the local chiefs, built himself a capital in Cooch Behār. The Koch tribe, though now in parts much intermixed with Dravidian stock, was probably at that time purely Mongolian and spoke a language closely allied to those of the Kacháris, Tipperas, Lalungs, Chutiyás, and Gáros. Biswa Singh was succeeded by his son Nar Nārāyan, who extended his kingdom in all directions. He defeated, among others, the chiefs of Dimaruá, Jaintiá, Khairam, Cáchár, and Tippera, and also the Ahom Rájá, whose capital he occupied until pacified by presents, hostages, and a promise of tribute. He met his match, however, in Isa Khán, the Muhammadan chief or Bhuiya of Sonārgaon in eastern Bengal, who defeated his army and took prisoner his brother Sukladhwaj, to whose military genius he had been mainly indebted for his successes elsewhere. In 1581 the latter's son, Raghu, having rebelled, was given the country east of the Sankosh, Nar Náráyan retaining for himself the portion west of that river, where he was succeeded on his death, in 1584, by his son Lakshmī Nārāyan. This dismemberment of the kingdom quickly led to its dissolution, but we must first deal with the state of things in other parts of the Brahmaputra Valley.

Early in the thirteenth century an event occurred at the eastern extremity of the valley which was destined to change the whole course of Assam history. This was the invasion of the Ahoms, a Shan tribe from the ancient kingdom of Mungmau or Pong, which was situated in the upper portion of the Irrawaddy valley.* A quarrel as to the right of succession to the throne is said to have been the cause of the secession of Sukapha, one of the rival claimants, who, after wandering about the country between the Irrawaddy and the Pātkai mountains for some years, crossed the range in 1228 with a small following and entered the tract which now forms the southern part of the Lakhimpur District and the south-east of Sibsāgar. It was at that time inhabited by petty tribes of Bodo affinities (Morans and Borahis), who were easily subdued: the country round Sadiyā, the northern part of the headquarters subdivision of Lakhimpur and the north-eastern part of Sibsāgar as far as the Disáng river, which had previously been governed by a line of Pāl kings, were under the rule of the Chutiyās, who had established a kingdom of considerable power; while the Kachāris occupied the western part of Sibsāgar, the valley of the Dhansiri and the greater part of the Nowgong District. Sukapha, finding his further progress barred, settled down among the Morans and Borahis, who were gradually absorbed into the Ahom community, a process that was accelerated by frequent intermarriages due to the paucity of Ahom women. In this way, aided probably by fresh streams of immigration from Pong, the Ahoms increased rapidly in numbers and power. Early in the fourteenth century there is a vague reference to a war with a Rájá of Kámata, who, it is said, was forced to sue for peace. A few years later the Ahoms became involved in a war with the Chutiyās. In 1376 the latter pretended to make peace, and then treacherously murdered the Ahom king, Sutupha, at a regatta on the Safrai river, held to celebrate the cessation of hostilities. This led to a renewal of the war; the Chutiyás were worsted, but their final overthrow did not take place until 1523, when Suhunmung, otherwise known as the Dihingia Rájá, who reigned from 1497 to 1539, utterly defeated them with heavy slaughter and annexed their country which he placed in charge of an Ahom viceroy called the Sadiyá-khowa Gohain: a number of Ahoms from Gargaon were settled at Sadiyá, while the leading families of the Chutiyās were deported to a place not far from Tezpur, and many of their artisans were brought to the Ahom capital. Meanwhile, there had been numerous expeditions against various Nágá tribes, which were generally successful, and, in 1490, the first war with the Kacháris, by whom the Ahoms were defeated on the banks of the Dikho river. This set-back was,

The Ahoms.

* The account here given of the Ahom kings is based mainly on manuscript *Buranjis*, or histories written in the Ahom language and character on strips of bark of the *sáchi* or *agar* tree (*Aquilaria agallocha*). In former times all the leading families had their own *Buranjis*, which were written up from time to time; many of these have disappeared, but a number still survive, and translations of these have been prepared.

however, only temporary, and little more than 30 years afterwards we find the Dihingia Rájá, whose victory over the Chutiyás has just been mentioned, fighting with the Kacháris on the bank of the Dhansiri. The Kacháris won a few minor successes, but in the end they were utterly vanquished. Their king was deposed and a new ruler named Detsung installed in his place. In 1536 hostilities again broke out; Detsung was taken and killed; his capital at Dimāpur was sacked; and the Kacháris were shorn of all their possessions in the valley of the Dhansiri and north of the Kalang river in Nowgong.

Muhammadan invasions. The Dihingia Rájá, like so many Ahom kings, met his death at the hands of an assassin, who was instigated, it is said, by his own son. His reign is memorable, not only for the extirpation of Chutiyá and Kachári rule from the valley of the Brahmaputra and (it is alleged) for the acknowledgment of his supremacy by the Koch king Biswa Singh, but also for the repulse of two Muhammadan expeditions. The second of these, in 1532, was led by a commander named Turbak, who worsted the Ahoms in several engagements, but was at last utterly defeated on the bank of the Bhareli river. He himself was slain with large numbers of his followers, and many were taken prisoners and settled in the Ahom country: these are reputed to be the ancestors of the Moriás. The use of fire-arms by the Ahoms dates from the close of this war. These two expeditions, though the first in which they are recorded to have come into collision with the Ahoms, were not by any means the earliest invasions by Muhammadans of country now included within the Province of Assam. In 1384 they had conquered and annexed Sylhet, excluding the submontane tracts in the north and south which were held by the Jaintiás and Tipperas, and at an even earlier date they had begun to harry the lower portion of the Brahmaputra Valley; but here, though their superior arms and discipline generally brought them a temporary success, their expeditions all ended in failure, induced by disease, ignorance of the country, the difficulty of communications, especially during the rainy season, and the impossibility of bringing up reinforcements to repair losses.

Expansion of the Ahom dominions. The power of the Ahoms continued to grow and their dominions to expand, and there was almost constant warfare between them and one or other of their neighbours--Narás,* Nágás, Kacháris, and Koch. They were nearly always successful, but sustained a crushing defeat at the hands of the Koch king Nar Náráyan, whose capture of the Ahom capital has already been referred to. Their recovery from this reverse was, however, extraordinarily rapid, and a fresh turn in the wheel of fortune soon gave them their revenge.

* The Narás occupied the country round Mogaung on the other side of the Pátkai. They are commonly regarded as Shans, but Ney Elias thought that they included in their composition a large aboriginal element.

Koch affairs after Nar Narayan's death.

Nar Nārāyan was succeeded in the western Koch kingdom by his son Lakshmī Nārāyan, who soon became embroiled with Parīkshit, the son of Raghu and his successor in the eastern kingdom. Being unable to hold his own, Lakshmī Nárāyan invoked the aid of the Muhammadans, who took Parīkshit's fort at Dhubri and soon afterwards invested his capital at Barnagar on the Manás. Parīkshit held out there for a time, but was at last forced to surrender and was sent a prisoner to Delhi, while his brother Bali Nārāyan fled to the Ahom king Pratāp Singh, who refused to give him up.

Fresh war between the Ahoms and the Muhammadans.

The Muhammadans, therefore, invaded the Ahom country with a force of from 10 to 12 thousand horse and foot and 400 large ships. They gained a victory near the mouth of the Bhareli river, but were soon afterwards annihilated in a night attack. Pratáp Singh thereupon installed Bali Nárāyan as successor to Parīkshit, and advanced and took Pandu near Gauhāti, which he fortified. He next laid siege to Hájo, but was driven back. The war dragged on in lower Assam for some years with varying success, but in 1637 the Nawāb of Dacca determined to take more vigorous measures, and he despatched what was practically a new army. This measure met with immediate success. The Ahoms were driven out of Kámrúp, Bali Nárāyan was killed, and a treaty was made by which the BARNADI was taken as the boundary between Ahom and Muhammadan territory.

Ahom conquest of lower Assam.

The Koch kings continued to rule west of the Sankosh as vassals of the Muhammadans, but when Shāh Jahān fell sick in 1658, Prān N rāyan, who was then on the throne, took advantage of the confusion ensuing on the wars of succession to throw off his allegiance, and defeated the Muhammadan *faujdar* of Goálpára. The latter retreated to Gauháti, but was driven thence by the Ahom king Jayadhwaj Singh. Prān Nárāyan proposed to the latter a friendly division of lower Assam, but his overtures were rejected and he was soon compelled to retreat beyond the Sankosh. The whole of the Brahmaputra valley thus fell into the hands of the Ahoms.

Mir Jumla's invasion.

When order was restored in Bengal, and Mír Jumla became governor at Dacca, he first attacked and defeated Prān Nár yan, and then advanced against the Ahoms, with an army, according to their writers, of 12,000 horse and 30,000 foot and a powerful fleet. The Ahoms were worsted both on land and water, and were gradually driven back. In spite of the great difficulty of locomotion due to the numerous watercourses and the vast expanse of dense jungle, Mír Jumla marched steadily up the south bank of the Brahmaputra, his fleet keeping pace with his army, and at last occupied Gargaon, the Ahom capital, where he halted for the wet season, which was now close at hand. The rains set in with unexampled severity, and the country soon became a quagmire. Supplies were hard to get and the Ahoms harassed the Mughals by repeated night attacks, and destroyed some outlying garrisons and isolated detachments. As the rains progressed, the position of the Muhammadans became more and more trying, and to the terrors of a persistent but unseen enemy were added severe epidemics of disease, especially dysentery. Mīr Jumla himself did not escape. Broken in health, he found himself unable to resist the clamour of his troops to be led back to Bengal: early in the cold weather a treaty was patched up, and he hurried back to Dacca, where he died soon afterwards. The Muhammadan historians have left on record an interesting account of their opponents. Their resources were considerable, and in the course of the expedition the Musalmāns captured more than one thousand war sloops from the enemy, many of which could accommodate from three to four score sailors. They also took nearly 700 guns, some of them of considerable size. Extensive fortifications had been erected on both sides of the river near Tezpur, and the country between Kaliābar and Gargaon was said to be well cultivated and adorned with gardens and orchards. Gargaon itself was a town of considerable size, and the historian waxes enthusiastic over the splendours of the Rájá's palace. The genuine Ahoms are described as keen and fearless soldiers, but their number was not large, and the Kalitā levies were of very small account. The Ahoms lost no time in retaking the country they had lost, and two years later we find them in undisputed possession of the whole of Kámrúp, and the advance guard of the Mughals located at Rangámáti in the Goálpára District.* For a time, however, internal troubles and a long series of conspiracies threatened to do that which external aggression had failed to effect, and in the brief space of eleven years there were no less than seven Ahom kings, not one of whom died a natural death. The Muhammadans took advantage of these disturbances to recover possession of Gauháti, but they were finally driven out in the reign of Gadadhar Singh, who ascended the throne in 1681.

Ahom wars with Kacharis and Jaintias.

The next king, Rudra Singh, being free from all fear of Muhammadan invasion and secure in his possession of Kámrúp, began to extend his kingdom in other directions. He took the south of Nowgong from the Kachāris and occupied Maibang in the North Cāchār hills, whither they had removed their capital on being ousted from Dimāpur. He also contemplated an invasion of their dominions in the Cáchár plains, which one of their Rájás had obtained as a gift from a Tippera king on the occasion of his marriage with the latter's daughter, but his troops suffered so much from sickness during the rainy season that

* Not the least interesting of the relics of this period is a cannon at Dikom bearing two inscriptions, the one in Persian stating that it had been made for use in the conquest of Assam, and the other in Sanskrit recording the fact that the Ahoms had taken it from the Muhammadans in battle.

he was obliged to desist. Meanwhile, the Kachári king, Tamradhwaj, had invoked the aid of the Jaintiás, a section of the Khási tribe, inhabiting the eastern part of the Khási and Jaintiá Hills who at this time also held the country between the foot of the hills and the Surmá river, and whose king, Rám Singh, had his headquarters at Jaintiápur in the same tract. On learning of the departure of the Ahoms, Tamradhwaj informed Rám Singh that his help was no longer needed, but the latter treacherously seized him and annexed his territory. Tamradhwaj managed to send word to Rudra Singh begging for his help, and the latter despatched two armies to Jaintiápur, one across the Jaintiá Hills and the other through the Kachári country. Both reached their destination; Jaintiápur was taken without difficulty; but when Rudra Singh's intention to bring them permanently under his yoke became known, the Jaintiás rose to a man, and his generals, finding their position untenable, were forced to beat a retreat.

Conversion of Ahoms to Hinduism.

Rudra Singh's reign is memorable for the final triumph of Hinduism over the national religion of the Ahoms.* Many of his predecessors had taken Hindu, as well as Ahom, names, and had shown great respect for the Brâhmans, but Rudra Singh was the first to publicly announce his intention to become the disciple of a Hindu priest. His son and successor, Sib Singh, was completely in the hands of Brâhmans of the Sâkta sect, and he allowed his wife, Phuleswari, at their instigation, to insult the Súdra Mahant of the Vaisbnava sect of Moamarias,† who had now become very numerous, by causing his forehead to be smeared with the blood of an animal that had been sacrificed to Durgá. The common people soon followed the lead of their king, and in a few years the Deodhais and Bailongs, the tribal priests and astrologers, alone remained true to the ancient faith of the Ahoms. The change was disastrous; it involved the loss of the old martial spirit and pride of race with which the Ahoms had till then been animated; their patriotic feelings thenceforth became more and more subordinated to sectarian animosities and internal dissensions and intrigues, and their power soon began to decay. In 1766 we read, for the first time, of Ahom nobles declining the proffered command of a military expedition.

Moamaria rebellions and consequent anarchy.

In 1769, soon after the accession of Lakshmi Singh, the Vaishnava Moamarias, enraged by fresh insults, rose in rebellion,

* The Ahoms were not mere Animists of the type commonly found among the aboriginal tribes of India, but had a regular pantheon of which the leading members were, in later times at least, identified with Hindu gods and goddesses. An account of the Ahom story of the creation will be found in a paper contributed by Mr. E. A. Gait to the Journal of the Asiatic Society of Bengal for 1894, and a translation of their cosmogony, with the Ahom text, is given by Dr. G. A. Grierson in the Journal of the Royal Asiatic Society for 1904.

† The Moamarias are a Vaishnavite sect, most of whose members are drawn from the lower Hindu castes and are residents of upper Assam. Three explanations of the origin of the name are current. According to one the original founder lived near the Moamari bhil in Nowgong, according to the other the people were called Moamaria in contempt because they were in the habit of catching and eating the Moa fish, while others say that the original Gosain Aniruddha convinced the Ahom king of the truth of the new religion by a display of magic *maya*.

seized the person of the king, and placed the son of a Matak* chief on the throne. For a time the rebels seemed to have overborne all opposition, but the report that their leader was contemplating the execution of all the old officers of state incited the royalists to renewed efforts. The Moamaria commander was killed in a night attack, and many of his chief supporters were put to death. Deprived of their leaders, the rebels offered but a feeble resistance, and they were easily dispersed. Lakshmī Singh died in 1780, and the accession of his son Gaurináth Singh was the signal for renewed persecutions. These led to fresh risings, and at last, in 1786, the rebels defeated the royal troops in several encounters and took the capital by storm. Gaurināth fled to Gauháti, but resistance was continued by one of his ministers, known as the Bura Gohain, and for several years the war dragged on with varying success. A general state of anarchy supervened; the country side was devastated by bands of armed men, and petty chiefs in all directions began to proclaim themselves independent. Among the latter was Krishna Náráyan, a descendant of the Koch kings, who seized Darrang and the northern part of Kámrúp and threatened Gauháti. The Moamarias also were advancing nearer and nearer.

British intervention in aid of the Ahom king.

Gaurināth now sought aid from the British, who had succeeded to the Mughals in Sylhet and Goálpára, and urged that his plight was due largely to the fact that Krishna Náráyan had been allowed to recruit men for his army in the Rangpur District. Lord Cornwallis recognised the obligation, and in September 1792 sent Captain Welsh with a small force to the Ahom king's relief. A little below Gauháti he was met by Gaurināth, who had fled from the city before a mob of Doms led by a Bairági. Welsh had no difficulty in driving them out, and he then crossed the Brahmaputra with 250 sepoys and defeated Krishna Náráyan's army of 3,000 men. After some further reverses the latter surrendered and his Bengal clubmen were deported. In his efforts to conciliate Gauráth's numerous enemies, Welsh found himself thwarted by the cruel and sanguinary conduct of the Rájá, and by the intrigues and covert opposition of some of his ministers. He replaced the latter by others of a more humane disposition, caused a general amnesty to be proclaimed, and took such other steps as seemed needed to restore confidence and ensure good government. He spent the rainy season of the year 1793 at Gauháti, and in January 1794, after pacifying Mangaldai and Nowgong, advanced to Kaliábar. Jorhát, where the Bura Gohain was still holding out against the Moamarias, was relieved by a small force; and a decisive victory was gained about twelve miles from Rangpur, which was occupied in March.

* The Mataks were the inhabitants of Lakhimpur and were so called because the raiding Singphos found them "Matak" or strong in contradistinction to the "Mullong" or weak people further east.

Sir John Shore had now succeeded Lord Cornwallis as Governor General, and one of his first acts was to recall Captain Welsh in spite of the vigorous protests of the Ahom king. The latter, when left once more to his own devices, dismissed most of the officials who had been appointed on Welsh's recommendation, renewed the persecution of the Moamarias and wreaked his vengeance on his old enemies who had made their submission under a promise of pardon, and for a time it seemed likely that Assam would once more relapse into anarchy. This was prevented by the energy of the Bura Gohain, who organized a body of troops disciplined on the English model, and, with their aid, the Moamarias and other malcontents were held in check.

The Burmese conquer the Ahoms.

Shortly after the accession of Chandra Kanta,* in 1810, the Ahom governor at Gauhāti fell into disgrace, and fled for safety to Calcutta. After seeking in vain the assistance of the British, he gained the friendship of the Burmese envoy to the Governor General and went with him to Amarapura, where he persuaded the Burmese king to send an expedition to Assam. In 1816-17 an army of 8,000 men was despatched from Burma, and, having crossed the Pátkai and gained fresh adherents among the hill chiefs, entered Assam, occupied the whole country as far as Jorhát, and reinstated the Gauháti governor. The force then returned to Burma. They had barely departed when fresh dissensions took place; the governor, who had invoked the aid of the Burmese, was assassinated; Chandra Kanta was deposed, and Purandar Singh, a direct descendant of Rájá Rājeswar Singh, was installed in his place. The friends of the late governor appealed to the Burmese, who once more appeared on the scene and reinstated Chandra Kanta, but on this occasion it soon became clear that they meant to stay. Chandra Kanta made a vain effort to throw off their yoke and fled to British territory, where Purandar Singh had frequently taken refuge. The Burmese during their occupation of the country treated the unfortunate inhabitants with extreme barbarity. The villages were plundered and burnt, and the inhabitants were driven into the jungle to live as best they could.

They are driven out by the British.

The gradual decline of the Ahom power had caused a relaxation of their pressure on the Kachári kings, whose capital was now at Khāspur in the plains of Cáchár, but the latter soon found a a fresh enemy on their eastern frontier, where the Manipurís became so threatening that, from 1817 onwards, constant appeals

* Gaurináth was followed by a very distant connection named Kamaleswar, a descendant of Gadadhar Singh, and Chandra Kanta, the next king, was Kamaleswar's brother. In the early days of Ahom rule the succession devolved from father to son with great regularity, but in later times brothers often succeeded to the exclusion of sons, and sometimes, as in the case of Kamaleswar, even very distant relations did so. Much depended on the wishes of the previous king, much on the action of the great nobles, with whom, in theory at least, the choice seems to have rested, and much on the personal influence of the rival candidates. The one absolutely essential qualification was that they must be of the royal blood. The per[illegible] the monarch was sacred and any marked blemish, even the scar of a carbuncle, op[illegible]d as a disqualification. Hence arose the practice, often followed by Ahom kings, of mut[illegible]ing all likely rivals. Mutilation was usually effected by slitting the ear.

for help had been made to the British. These were rejected until early in 1824, when intelligence of a projected invasion of Cáchár and Jaintiá by the Burmese led the British Government, who had received great provocation from Burma in other quarters, to intervene. Our first collision with Burmese troops occurred on the Cáchár frontier, but the scene of the main operations in Assam was in the Brahmaputra Valley, where a British force of 3,000 men advanced without much opposition as far as Kaliābar. On the approach of the rainy season the troops returned to Gauháti, and the Burmese re-occupied Nowgong, where they committed terrible atrocities on the helpless inhabitants. Many were put to death and many fled for their lives into the hills to the south; of the latter, the majority died of starvation, and only a small remnant lived to reach the plains of the Surmá Valley. When the rains were over, the British again advanced, and the Burmese were driven out of the Province after a few fainthearted and ineffectual attempts at resistance, but in the course of their retreat they carried off as slaves upwards of 30,000 Assamese.

Incorporation of Assam in British dominions. Gradual expansion of Province.

By the treaty of Yandabo in 1826 the Burmese ceded Assam to the East India Company, and Mr. Scott, the Commissioner of Rangpur, was appointed to administer the country. The Moamarias in the south of the Lakhimpur District were left under their own ruler, the Bor Senápati, and the Sadiyá-khowa Gohain or Khamti chief of Sadiyá, who had dispossessed the Ahoms there during the Moamaria rebellions, was confirmed as the Company's feudatory in that tract, while, in 1833, the rest of the Lakhimpur District and Sibságar were restored to Purandar Singh. These arrangements, however, did not last long. In 1838 Purandar Singh declared himself unable to carry on the administration, and his territory was taken over. In 1835 the Sadiyá-khowá Gohain was removed from his post; but the local Khamti chiefs were allowed to manage their own internal affairs till 1839, when, without any warning, they made a night attack on the garrison of Sadiyá, and killed Colonel White, the officer in command, and a number of his sepoys; the Khamtis were then deported to places lower down the river, and the power of their chiefs was finally extinguished. In 1842 the Bor Senāpati died, and on his son declining to accept the terms of settlement offered to him, his country also was annexed.

In Cáchár the lawful Rájá was replaced on the throne, but was soon forced to relinquish the northern portion of his domains to a rebel named Tula Rám. The Rájá was assassinated in 1830 and, in the absence of any lawful heir, the Cáchár plains were annexed to British territory. Five years later Tula Rám ceded a considerable tract of territory, and the rest of his country was taken over soon after his death in 1850, as his sons had proved unable to manage it. In 1835 the Rájá of Jaintiā was dispossessed of his estate in the plains, in consequence of the repeated abduction of British subjects who were sacrificed to Kālī, the tutelary goddess of his family. He then declared himself unwilling to continue in possession of his hill territory, over which he had but little control, and it also was included in the Company's dominions. The Khāsi Hills to the west were conquered in 1832, as the result of an attack made on a party engaged in constructing a road through the hills, but the people were left in a state of *quasi*-independence under their own chiefs, with the exception of a few villages which were acquired for special reasons, either at the time of the conquest or at some subsequent date: among the latter may be mentioned the site of Shillong, the capital of the Province as now constituted. Our occupation of the Nágá Hills has been a gradual process due to the necessity of protecting British subjects from Nágá raids. It commenced in 1866, when a frontier District was formed, with headquarters at Sámaguting, and the last addition was made in 1904 when the eastern Angāmī country was formally annexed. Theoretically, the Gáro Hills always formed part of the Goálpára District, but for many years our control over the Gáros was limited to ineffectual efforts to suppress their constant raids on the adjoining plains by means of punitive expeditions or by forbidding them to trade in the plains. In 1869 the tract was formed into a separate District, with headquarters at Turā, and order was instantly established in all but the more remote villages. The inhabitants of the latter, having perpetrated fresh raids, were brought under subjection in 1872-73 with the aid of a few small detachments of police, who met with no serious opposition. Prior to 1890, the history of our relations with the Lushais was one of constant raids by the latter, followed by infructuous punitive expeditions. In that year, after one of these expeditions, it was decided to try the expedient of establishing military outposts in their midst. A treacherous attack on two of these outposts led to fresh operations and to the permanent annexation of the Lushai Hills, which are now in charge of a Superintendent, with headquarters at Aijal.

The Manipur State has a fairly ancient history, but the present régime dates only from 1714, when the reigning chief adopted Hinduism, which has now gained a remarkably strong hold on the people. By the treaty of Yandabo, the Burmese agreed to the restoration to the throne of Rájá Gambhir Singh whom they had ousted. He and his descendants enjoyed a large measure of independence, and the British Government rarely interfered in local affairs except in the case of risings or disputes regarding the succession. In 1890, in the course of one of these risings, the Mahārājā was driven from his palace and abdicated in favour of the Jubrāj, but he subsequently repudiated his abdication. The

Manipur State.

Government of India decided to confirm the Jubrāj as Rájá, but directed the Chief Commissioner to arrest and deport the Senápati, who had been the ringleader in the plot. He proceeded to Manipur and called on the Senápati to surrender himself, but the latter refused to do so and resisted the troops sent to seize him. The Chief Commissioner and four other officers were then induced, under a promise of safe-conduct, to attend, alone and unarmed, a darbār in the palace. The discussion was infructuous and they started to return, but a crowd of Manipurīs closed in on them and two of them were wounded with spears. One died of his wound, and all the other officers, after a short detention, were cruelly murdered. This led to an expedition. Manipur was occupied by British troops; the ringleaders were punished; the new Rájá was deposed, and a scion of a collateral line was raised to the throne. Since this time a large measure of control has been vested in the resident British Officer, who is now designated "Political Agent and Superintendent of the State."

Chief Commissioners of Assam. Until 1874, Assam was administered as part of Bengal, but in that year it was formed into a separate Province under a Chief Commissioner. The officers who have held this appointment since that date are noted below :—

Colonel R. H. Keatinge	1874
Sir Steuart Bayley	1878
Mr. (afterwards Sir) Charles Elliott... ...	1881
Mr. (afterwards Sir) William Ward... ...	1885 Offg.
Mr. (afterwards Sir) Dennis Fitzpatrick ...	1887
Mr. (afterwards Sir) James Westland ...	1889
Mr. J. W. Quinton	1889
Sir William Ward	1891
Mr. (afterwards Sir) Henry Cotton	1896
Mr. J. B. Fuller	1902

NOTE.—Officiating appointments for less than six months are omitted.

Archæology. Assam is somewhat destitute of archæological remains of interest. The natives of the Province have little aptitude for handicrafts, and many of the temples that exist were probably constructed by artisans from Hindustán. The shrine of Shāh Jalál is situated in a mosque at Sylhet, which is still in an excellent state of preservation, and there are some interesting ruins at JAINTIAPUR. Kámrúp has many temples, but most of them are small and have fallen into disrepair, the two best known being the temple to KAMAKHYA on Nilúchal hill near Gauháti, and the temple of Hayagriva Mādhab at HAJO. There are also the remains of an interesting stone bridge in the Silā Sindurighopā mauza, which is said to have been constructed by

Bakhtiār Khiljī when he invaded Assam at the beginning of the 13th century. Near Tezpur are the ruins of what must once have been a magnificent stone temple, but not one stone is left standing upon another, and its builder and designer are alike unknown. DIMAPUR in the extreme south-western corner of the Sibsāgar District, was once the capital of the Kachári dynasty, and was evidently a place of considerable importance, though it is now situated in the centre of an enormous forest. Sibságar has numerous temples built by the Ahom kings. They are made of thin bricks of excellent quality, and are generally ornamented with bas-reliefs; but the fact that figures of camels not unfrequently appear suggests that they were erected under the direction of foreign artisans, as camels must always have been very scarce in a damp and marshy country like Assam. These temples have been generally built on the side of large tanks, whose construction must have entailed an enormous expenditure of labour. The largest tank, at Sibsāgar, covers an area of 114 acres. Immense tanks, with temples on their banks, have also been constructed at Gauriságar, Rudraságar and Jayságar, all within a few miles of the Sibságar tank. At Gargaon near NAZIRA are the ruins of one of the Ahom capitals. That the native rulers of Assam extended their frontiers right up to the Himālayas is shown by the remains of a fort at Bhálukpāng in the gorge of the Bhareli, and of two large forts some distance north of Sadiyá. Another interesting ruin near that place is the small temple at which a human victim was annually offered for many centuries by the Chutiyā priests. Scattered about the valley are the remains of great roads and fortifications which evidently protected the capital of some local prince. The Baidargarh in Kámrúp, which is said to have been constructed by king Arimatta about the 13th century A.D., and his son Jangal's fort in Nowgong, deserve special mention, as do also the remains of extensive earthworks at Pratāpgarh, near Bishnāth, in the Darrang District.

POPULATION.

General distribution.

The population of Assam, including the Native State of Manipur, returned at the census of 1901, amounted to 6,126,343 persons, living in 19 towns and 22,326 villages, and can be most conveniently considered with reference to the three natural divisions into which the Province falls.

Over the greater part of the Surmā Valley there is no longer any scarcity of population. In the Cáchár plains the density is only 201 to the square mile, but the country is much broken up by hills and marshes, and of recent years it has become necessary to throw open considerable areas of reserved forest to meet the demand for culturable land. The neighbouring District of Sylhet is fully peopled, and in the Habiganj subdivision the density rises to 583 to the square mile, which for a purely rural population must be considered high. In the Brahmaputra valley the condition of affairs is very different. Though three times the size of the valley of the Surmā, it supports a slightly smaller population, and the density in its Districts varies from 68 in Nowgong to 153 in Kāmrūp. A considerable portion of the unsettled area consists of steep jungle-covered hills, and of marshes that could only grow cold-weather crops or the longest-stemmed varieties of rice; but much good land remains awaiting settlement, and there is probably room for another two or three million inhabitants. There are, however, places where the population is already fairly dense, and in certain rural tracts in the centre of Kāmrūp and Sibsāgar it exceeds 600 to the square mile. The hill Districts are very sparsely peopled, but the area of land suited for permanent cultivation is small, and large tracts of waste are required for the support of tribes that live by shifting cultivation.

Towns and villages.

The population of Assam is almost entirely rural, and, excluding Manipur, less than 2 per cent. of the people enumerated in 1901 were living in urban areas. The largest towns were SYLHET (13,893), GAUHATI (11,661), DIBRUGARH (11,227), SILCHAR (9,256), BARPETA (8,747), and SHILLONG, the headquarters of the Administration, (8,384). Many of the towns are little more than large villages, and the average population of 18 places dignified with that name was only 6,315. Imphal, the capital of Manipur, had a population of 67,093, but the rural character of the place is illustrated by the fact that more than half of the working males residing there were agriculturists by profession. Except in the Nāgā, North Cáchár, and Lushai Hills, the boundaries of a village are not clearly defined, and the cottages are scattered over a considerable area. This tendency is particularly marked in the Assam Valley. Rice is grown on broad plains, which are often several miles in length and which are dotted over with clumps of bamboos and fruit trees in which are buried the houses of the cultivators. A village, in the sense of a compact block of houses set in the midst of its fields at a considerable distance from any other little centre of population, is the exception rather than the rule in the plains of Assam, and for census purposes a village was taken to be the area so designated by the cadastral survey party. In many cases, however, the cadastral village is little more than a tract of land which can conveniently be surveyed on one sheet of the map, and this fact has to be borne in mind when examining the statistics showing their average size. In Sylhet there is so little high land that the people are compelled to live in fairly close proximity, but all over the Province there is a marked preference for small hamlets. In 1901, 56 per cent. of the population were living in villages of less than 500 inhabitants, 38 per cent. in those ranging from 500 to 2,000, and less than 5 per cent. in those containing from 2,000 to 5,000 people.

Growth of population. The first regular census was taken in 1872, and disclosed a population of 4,150,769 souls. Manipur and the Lushai Hills were not included, and the figures for the hill Districts were only estimates. In 1881, the population, including Manipur, was 5,128,862; and in the plains alone there was an increase of over 18 per cent., a fact which threw grave doubts on the accuracy of the former enumeration. In 1891, Manipur again dropped out, the census schedules having been destroyed in the rising, but the Lushai Hills appeared for the first time, and the population was returned at 5,477,302. The population of the plains increased by nearly 11 per cent., but part of this increase was no doubt due to the greater accuracy of the enumeration in 1891. In the last intercensal period the increase was 649,041, or 12 per cent., but this was largely due to the inclusion of figures for Manipur and the South Lushai Hills, and in the plains the increase was less than 6 per cent. The year 1897 was very unhealthy and in central and lower Assam an abnormal mortality was not confined to that year alone. The population of Kāmrūp decreased by over 7 per cent., and, though there was an increase in Darrang, it was entirely due to immigration, and the indigenous inhabitants are believed to have decreased by 8 per cent. The lowest depth was, however, reached in Nowgong, where the people were more than decimated by a peculiarly malignant form of malarial fever known as *kalá-ázár*. The population of the District as a whole fell by nearly one-fourth, and it was calculated that the indigenous inhabitants had decreased by over 30 per cent. In upper Assam there was a satisfactory growth of the indigenous population, and an enormous development of immigration during the decade. The population of Sibsāgar increased by nearly one-fourth, and that of Lakhimpur by almost a half. The best indication of the natural growth of the people is, however, obtained by excluding the figures for Manipur and the Lushai Hills, and comparing the figures for those born and enumerated in the Province in 1891 and 1901. Among this class it appears that the increase during the last intercensal period was only a little more than one per cent.

Immigrants. There was, however, a great growth of the immigrant population, which increased by more than one-half, and in 1901 exceeded three-quarters of a million, or nearly 13 per cent. of the total population of the Province. The great bulk of these foreigners are coolies brought up to the tea gardens, though a certain amount of movement takes place across the frontier where Assam marches with Bengal. More than half a million people came from that Province, a quarter of a million of whom were born in the Division of Chotā Nāgpur. About 109,000 persons came from the United Provinces, and 84,000 from the Central Provinces. The preponderance of the foreign-born element in the population was most pronounced in Lakhimpur, where they formed 41 per cent. of the whole, and Darrang and Sibsāgar (25 per cent.) Cāchār (plains) was close behind, with 24 per cent. In Sylhet, on the other hand, though the total number of foreigners was considerable, they only formed 7 per cent. of the population. There is very little emigration, and only 51,000 persons born in Assam were found in other parts of India. The great majority of these persons had only crossed the frontier from Goālpāra and Sylhet into Bengal.

Age. Little reliance can be placed upon the age statistics, as only a small proportion of the population have even an approximate idea of the number of years which they have lived, and though the mistakes made tend to some extent to neutralize one another, there is a marked tendency to select multiples of five. Inaccurate though the figures are, they show that the exceptional unhealthiness which prevailed between 1891 and 1901 affected the fecundity of the people, and the decrease in the proportion of children was especially pronounced in Districts like Nowgong and the Khāsi Hills, where the death rate was exceptionally high. The most prolific section of the people includes the animistic tribes, and it seems possible that the system of early marriage may have a prejudicial effect upon the reproductive powers of Hindu women.

Vital statistics and prevalent diseases. The registration of vital statistics is only compulsory on tea gardens, and in the District and subdivisional headquarters stations in the plains (population, 1901, 765,000), but attempts are made to collect information in all the plains Districts and in a small portion of the hills. In Goālpāra the returns are submitted in writing by the village *panchāyats* and are fairly correct. In the Surmā Valley vital statistics are reported by the paid village chaukīdārs, and their accuracy leaves much to be desired. In Assam proper they are collected by the gaonburas or village headmen, and are extremely incomplete. The mean annual birth rate of the plains Districts during the five years ending with 1902 was only 33 per mille, and varied from 42 in Goālpāra, where public health had been bad, to 25 in Sibsāgar and Lakhimpur, where it had been good. The mean death rate was 30 per mille and varied from 41 in Nowgong to 21 in Sibsāgar. The returns have thus but little absolute value, though as the amount of error is fairly constant, they afford some clue to the comparative unhealthiness of different years. The sanitary conditions of Assam are far from satisfactory. The tract at the foot of the hills and the valleys running up into them are excessively malarious; and as the Province practically consists of two valleys with the intervening range, the proportion of this feverish tarai land is higher than in other parts of India. On the other hand, the open country is fairly healthy, and though the climate is damp it is also cool. The most prevalent diseases are fever, bowel complaints, pulmonary affections, cholera, worms, small-pox, various cutaneous disorders, and, in some localities, goitre. Leprosy is by no means uncommon, and in 1901 more than 5,000 persons were said to be afflicted with this disease. The birth and death-rates in 1881 and subsequent years and the mortality ascribed to the principal diseases, are shown in the following abstract:—

Year.	Population under registration.	Ratio of registered births per 1,000.	Ratio of registered deaths per 1,000.	Deaths per 1,000 from			
				Cholera.	Small-pox.	Fever.	Bowel complaints.
1881	4,483,705*	19	16	1	1	9	2
1891	5,021,084	29	30	5	...	15	3
1901	5,275,706	34	28	1	1	16	2
1903	5,275,706	36	27	2	...	14	2

* This is the population amongst whom deaths were registered. Births were only registered amongst a population of 2,225,271.

These rates do not represent the actual mortality due to these different ailments, but give a fairly correct idea of their comparative importance.

Kalá-ázár and plague.

The most important factor in the medical history of the Province during the last twenty years has, however, been *kalá-ázár*. The disease was known as far back as 1869, when it was reported to be an intense form of malarial fever which was inducing a high rate of mortality in the low and densely-wooded Gāro Hills, but first came into prominence in 1883, when it entered that portion of the Goālpāra District which lies south of the river. In 1888, it spread to Kāmrūp, and thence to Nowgong and to Mangaldai on the north bank of the Brahmaputra, and of recent years it has reached the district of Sylhet. The virulence of the epidemic is now gradually abating, and it has as yet failed to effect a lodgment in upper Assam, but it has been the cause of terrible mortality in the Districts it attacked. Between 1881 and 1891 the population of the Goālpāra subdivision decreased by 18 per cent.; and the population recorded in Kāmrūp in 1891 was estimated to have been less by 75,000 people than it would have been had there been no deaths from *kalá-ázár*. In the next decade the population of Kâmrûp decreased by 7 per cent., that of the Mangaldai subdivision of Darrang by 9 per cent., of the Nowgong District by 25 per cent., and of the North Sylhet subdivision by 4 per cent., and the excessive mortality indicated by these figures was, at any rate in the Assam Valley, chiefly due to this disease. Its nature is still a cause of speculation to the medical world. In all essentials it seemed to be a form of malarial fever, but the suggestion that malarial fever could be infectious was till recently opposed to all the accepted theories on the subject. Subsequently, it was thought that *kálá-ázár* was only an acute form of malarial poisoning, the difference between it and ordinary fever lying in the rapidity with which it produces a condition of severe cachexia, the small proportion of recoveries, and the ease with which it can be communicated from the sick to the healthy. Quite recently, the malarial theory of origin has been again assailed and the whole question is still involved in much uncertainty. Persons attacked seldom died in less than three months, and often lingered for two years, and isolation and segregation were thus impossible, once the disease had obtained a foothold. Plague did not appear in Assam till the rainy season of 1903, when it broke out among the foreign grain merchants in Dibrugarh. The disease was quickly stamped out and only 28 deaths occurred. The age statistics recorded at the census and the vital statistics supplied by the collecting agency are so inaccurate that it is impossible to place any reliance on the recorded death rate for infants under one year of age. It is, however, generally supposed to be about 218 per mille.

Every census in Assam has disclosed a deficiency of women and in 1901 there were only 949 females to every thousand males. This deficiency was to some extent due to the disproportion between the sexes among immigrants; and for those born and enumerated in the Province there were 977 women to every 1,000 men. Among the animistic tribes women usually predominate, and, taking those born in the hill Districts and enumerated in the Province, the proportion was 1,061 females to 1,000 males. This phenomenon is probably due in part to the practice of adult marriage, and in part to the good position usually assigned to women in the hills. In Nowgong it appears that there was some truth in the popular idea that *kalá-asár* spared the female members of the family, as at the last census, among those born and enumerated in the District, the women exceeded the men in numbers. The shortage of women was most pronounced in Sibságar and Lakhimpur, where there were only 886 and 862 females to every 1,000 males. This was partly due to an actual deficiency of women among the indigenous inhabitants, partly to the large foreign element in the population.

Marriage.

In Assam, as in other parts of India, wedlock is taken as a matter of course, and in 1901 more than half the population were either married, or had at any rate performed the ceremony at some period of their lives. Child marriage is common both among Hindus and Muhammadans in the Surmá Valley and Goálpārā, but in Assam proper, Bráhmans and Ganaks alone adhere rigidly to this rule, and the lower castes usually defer marriage till the girl is of an age to be able to enter on her new duties as wife and mother. Where adult marriage prevails, ante-nuptial chastity is not invariably demanded, and in Assam proper the marriage ceremony often consists of little more than a public acknowledgment of union, which does not receive the sanction of any priestly blessing. The purchase of a bride by service is also not uncommon, and during the time that the man is serving in the house of his prospective father-in-law, he is usually allowed free access to the girl of his choice. There is, however, a curious survival among the Kūkis which points to a time when this permission was not accorded. Pregnancy entails no disgrace, but on no account must a girl give birth to a living child in her father's house. At the seventh month the baby's head is crushed in the womb, and premature delivery is brought on, in spite of the fact that the process is attended with much risk to the young mother. The age of marriage among men depends largely upon the cost of the bride, and notwithstanding the easiness of the hill girl's morals, men marry early among the animistic tribes, as women are fairly numerous and therefore cheap. When the knot is once tied, the hill woman usually settles down and becomes an exemplary wife and mother, except among the Khásis, where divorces can be and are obtained on almost any pretext, and women not unfrequently change their husbands more than once. Such laxity in the marriage laws is bound to be accompanied by uncertainty as to the paternity of the children born, and it is doubtless for this reason that the Khāsi husband is not master in his own house, and that inheritance goes through the female line. Polygamy is nowhere common, as few men can afford the luxury of a second wife. Divorce is recognised by Muhammadans and the animistic tribes, and, in practice, by the lower castes of Hindus, unless the marriage has been contracted by the *hom pura* rite, which is looked upon as indissoluble.

The joint family system is far from prevalent in Assam proper, and even among the upper classes seldom extends beyond the second generation. In the Surmā Valley also it is the exception rather than the rule, and among the middle classes generally ends with the third generation.

The distribution of population by civil condition (for British territory only) is shown in the following table :—

Civil condition.	1891.			1901.		
	Persons.	Males.	Females.	Persons.	Males.	Females.
Unmarried ...	2,664,494	1,573,539	1,090,955	2,827,613	1,666,963	1,160,650
Married ...	2,207,826	1,110,525	1,097,301	2,366,952	1,194,774	1,172,178
Widowed ...	562,923	114,844	448,079	647,318	142,323	504,990

Language. The two main indigenous languages of the Province are Bengali, which was spoken by 48 per cent. of the population in 1901, and Assamese, which was returned by 22 per cent. Bengali is the common vernacular of the Surmá Valley, where it is used by 87 out of every 100 people, and of Goálpára (69 per cent.). Assamese is used by 83 per cent. of the inhabitants of Kámrúp; but in the tea Districts the proportion of foreigners is very large, and in Darrang it was returned by little more than half the population, and in Lakhimpur by only 39 per cent. In addition to the two main vernaculars, there are a large number of languages peculiar to Assam, most of which belong to the Tibeto-Burman stock, and which, though gradually giving place to Assamese, are still largely used. The most important were, Bodo or plains Kachári, Khási, Synteng, the various forms of Nágá dialects, Gáro, Manipurī, Lushai, Kúki, Mīkīr, and Mīrī. The principal foreign languages were Hindustáni, Mundāri, Santáli, and Oriyá. The number of persons in British territory who returned these different forms of speech is shown in the following table. Altogether, no less than 167 different languages were returned in Assam in 1901.

Language spoken.	1891.	1901.
Bengali	2,741,947	2,947,916
Assamese	1,414,285	1,349,694
Eastern Hindī, Western Hindī, and Hindustāni.	229,456*	351,908
Bodo, Dimasa, and Mech	269,346	237,982
Other languages	780,209	954,378†

* Figures for Hindi.

† Includes 123,481 Khási, 54,253 Syntengs, 106,035 Nágá, 133,411 Gáro, 72,011 Lushai, 82,283 Mikir, 40,472 Miri, 37,411 Mundāri, 30,128 Santali, and 23,758 Oriyá.

Tribe and caste.

The earliest inhabitants of Assam were probably the various offshoots of the great Indo-Chinese hordes, whose headquarters are said to have been on the upper waters of the Yang-tse-Kiang and Ho-ang-ho. At the same time, the Assam Valley must have been colonized by Hindus from the west at a very early date; and Hindu princes were reigning at the eastern end near Sadiyā at the time of the invasion of the Chutiyās, a tribe of Bodo origin, about a thousand years ago. The Chutiyās overthrew the Hindus, but in their turn gave way before the Ahoms, a Shan tribe who crossed the Pátkai from the kingdom of Pong in the 13th century, and gradually extended their sway over the whole valley. In the course of their expansion they overthrew the Koch kings, a dynasty of Bodo origin who had attained to considerable power and influence in north-eastern Bengal, and repulsed the Muhammadans, who made several attempts upon the valley and succeeded in holding for a considerable time the two lower Districts of Kāmrūp and Goálpára. The last wave of immigration was not one of either conquerors or colonists in the ordinary sense of the term, but of tea-garden coolies, who are now beginning to form an important element in the population of the upper Districts of the Assam Valley.

The Indo-Chinese tribes.

The various tribes of Indo-Chinese origin fall into several groups. The first are the Khásis, who are believed to be an isolated remnant of one of the earliest waves of migration from the north-east. They differ in many ways from all their neighbours, and on linguistic grounds it has been suggested that they may be connected with the Palaungs and Was in Upper Burma. The second great division includes the Dimasa or hill Kachári, the Bodo or plains Kachári, who are called Mech in Goálpára, the Rabhás, the Gāros, the Lalungs, and the eastern sub-Himálayan group consisting of the Daflās, Miris, Abors, and Mishmis. The Tipperas who occupy the hills south of Sylhet were also of Bodo stock, and there are good reasons for supposing that some of the earliest inhabitants of the Surmā Valley were members of this race. Another group comprises the Lushais and Kúkis, who have migrated from the south, and seem to be connected with the Manipuris; and the Nāgās, whose extraordinary ferocity differentiates them in some degree from the other hill tribes of the Province. The Mikirs are a peaceful tribe, whose language is akin both to Bodo and to Nāgā, but language is by no means a certain test of ethnical affinity. The Kacháris, Rabhás, and Meches live on the high grassy plains at the foot of the Himálayas, but most of the remainder occupy the hills of the Province. They are all of sturdy physique, and of a marked Mongolian type. They place few restrictions upon their natural appetites, and the warlike and aggressive spirit of the Gāros, Nāgās, and Lushāis for many years gave trouble to the Government. At the present day, many of the Nāgā tribes beyond the British frontier are still nothing more than bloodthirsty and naked savages. Another division of the Indo-Chinese inhabitants is a branch of the great Tai race, to which belong the Siamese and the Shans of Upper Burma. It includes the Ahoms, who have now to all intents and purposes become a Hindu caste, and several small colonies of Shans who have migrated into Assam in comparatively recent times. The strength of the principal tribes in 1901, was: Kachāris 240,000, Gāros 128,000, Rabhās 67,000, Meches 75,000, Mikīrs 87,000, Lalungs 36,000 Lushais 63,000, Kūkis 56,000, Manipurīs 256,000, Nāgās 162,000, Khāsis 178,000, and Mīris 47,000.

Hindu castes. Assam Proper. The natural result of the various changes outlined in the preceding paragraphs is that Hinduism in general, and caste in particular, are much less rigid in Assam than in Bengal. The first Hindu immigrants seem to have entered the valley of the Brahmaputra at a time when the boundary lines between one caste and another were not very clearly defined, and the presence of a large non-Hindu population, sections of which from time to time attained to sovereignty, made it impossible for them to affect too strict a standard of religious purity. The higher castes are thus somewhat lax in the observance of the ceremonial details of their religion; while castes, which in Bengal are of a comparatively low rank, enjoy in Assam a much more respectable position. Brāhmans and Kāyasthās are found in both valleys, but the most characteristic caste of Assam proper is the Kalitā. Various explanations have been put forward to account for the origin of this caste, which is almost peculiar to Assam, but it is now generally thought that they are the remains of a Hindu colony who settled in the Province at a time when the functional castes were still unknown. The Kalitās are divided into two main subdivisions, Bar and Saru, who do not usually intermarry, and there are various functional subdivisions which occupy a slightly lower position than the Bar Kalitā. The names Kewat and Kaibartta are used more or less indiscriminately for the same caste in Assam. Owing to the comparative scarcity of the higher castes, the cultivating Kewats occupy a higher position in this Province than in Bengal, but some of them have taken to styling themselves Māhisya Vaisya, as they resent the attempt on the part of the Nadiyāls or Doms to assume the name Kaibartta. The Koches were originally a tribe of Mongolian origin, who were the masters of lower Assam and north-eastern Bengal, till overthrown by the Muhammadans and Ahoms about the beginning of the 17th century. They are now, in lower Assam, a caste into which all converts to Hinduism are admitted. In Goālpāra the term Koch has been abandoned for the more honourable title Rājbansi—"men of royal race." The Sāloi are a respectable caste in Kāmrūp, who are believed to be connected with the Halwais, or confectioners, and the Patiās, most of whom are found in Nowgong, are theoretically mat-makers. Both of these castes have abandoned their traditional occupation and taken to agriculture. Of castes from whose hands water is not taken by Brāhmans, the principal is the Ahom. They were originally a Shan tribe, who entered Assam in the 13th century and settled in the Sibsāgar District. They overthrew successively the Chutiyā and the Koch, and eventually became masters of the Assam Valley. But they never colonised lower Assam, and the great bulk of the Chutiyās and Ahoms are still found in the Sibsāgar and Lakhimpur Districts. In the 17th century they were converted to Hinduism, and shortly afterwards the power of the tribe began to decline. The Jugis are theoretically weavers by profession, but most of them have taken to agriculture. The Nadiyāls or Doms are a fishing caste, and in Assam have never performed any of the degrading offices assigned to them in Bengal. They are cleanly in their persons, and great purists in the matter of their religion. The Boriā, or Sūt, are a caste peculiar to the Assam Valley. They are said to be the descendants of Brāhman widows and other persons who have contracted alliances not recognised by customary law.

Caste in the Surma Valley.

The characteristic castes of the Surmā Valley differ from those in Assam, though many are common to the two valleys. The great cultivating class of Sylhet are the Das (121,000), who often use the prefix Sūdra and Halwā. The Sūdras (46,000) are many of them members of the Das caste; but there is in Sylhet a genuine caste, that has no other name, composed of people who were formerly the slaves of Brāhmans (109,000) and Kāyasths (87,000). The members of the Navasākha, or respectable profession castes, most strongly represented, are the Telis, or oil-pressers' (39,000), the Goālās, or cowherds (38,000), the Nāpits, or barbers (32,000), the Baruis, or betel-leaf growers (12,000), the Kumhārs, or potters (27,000), and the Kamārs, or blacksmiths (34,000). The Baidyas (5,000) are theoretically doctors, and socially occupy a position immediately below the Brāhmans. The Shāhās (51,000) are by tradition liquor-sellers, but in Sylhet they are the chief trading caste, and many of them have amassed considerable wealth; in the Assam Valley they are ordinary cultivators, and Brāhmans take water from their hands. The Namasūdras, or Chandāls (170,000), are a fishing and boating caste. The foreign castes most numerous in 1901 were Baurīs (42,000), Bhuiyās (43,000), Bhumij (34,000), Chamārs (44,000), Ghātwāls (22,000), Kurmīs (21,000), Mundās (81,000), Oraons (24,000), and Santāls (78,000). Nearly all of these persons had originally been brought up to Assam to work on tea-gardens. The following castes are also numerically strong: Koches (222,000), Rājbansis (120,000), Kalitās (205,000), Nadiyāls (195,000), Ahoms (178,000), Jugis (161,000), Kewats (149,000), and Chutiyās (86,000).

Hinduism. Vaishnavism. Of the total population of the Province 3,429,099 persons, or 56 per cent., were returned as Hindus, more than half of whom professed the milder tenets of Vaishnavism. This form of Hinduism is especially prevalent in the Assam Valley, where its *gosains*, or principal priests, occupy positions of great influence and dignity. The *gosain* generally lives in a *sattra* or college, surrounded by his *bhokots*, or resident disciples. In some of the smaller *sattras* celibacy is not enforced, but in the larger colleges, neither the *gosain* nor the *bhokots* are allowed to marry. The *sattras* are not educational institutions like the Buddhist monasteries of Burma, nor do the inmates wander abroad into the neighbouring villages to solicit alms. The more important *sattras* hold grants of revenue-free land, which in some cases amount to several thousand acres, and all the non-resident disciples make an annual contribution towards their maintenance. The *gosain* of a large *sattra* is the spiritual head of a wealthy and powerful college, and is looked up to as the ultimate authority in religious and social matters by thousands of villagers, many of whom live miles away. In most of the larger *sattras* the presiding *gosain* is a Brāhman, but in some of the smaller institutions he is a Kalitā or Kāyasth. These priests are the great proselytizing agency in Assam; they exercise a civilizing influence on the aboriginal tribes, and have always been distinguished by their loyalty to Government and by an enlightenment and liberality of thought, which is not invariably found among the religious heads of a people. A special form of Vaishnavism found in the Assam Valley is the Mahāpurushia faith, which was founded by a Kāyasth named Sankar Deb, about the end of the 15th century, and represents a revolt against the pretentious claims of the Brāhmans, and the licentious rites of corrupted forms of Saktism. Its followers pay little attention to caste, are willing to accept a Sūdra as their *gosain*, are uncompromising in their hostility to idols, and worship God, in the form of Krishna, with hymns and prayers only. Sankar Deb himself was a vegetarian, but he was unable to impose this rule upon his followers, who were for the most part men of low caste, and they are allowed to eat the flesh of wild, but not of domesticated animals. The sect has a following of about 400,000, but the returns have to be accepted with a certain degree of caution.

Hindu. Nearly one-fifth of the Hindu population described themselves as followers of Sakti or Kālī, who represents the procreative force as manifested in the female. The temple of Kāmākhya in Kāmrūp is a special object of veneration to the devotees of this creed, as it is said to cover the place where the pudenda of Satī fell, when her body was cut in pieces by Vishnu; but Saktism, as a rule, is not popular with the inhabitants of Assam, and many of the so-called Saktists were merely garden coolies and rough tribesmen, who had not yet learned sufficient self-restraint to abandon meat and liquor. The devotees of Siva, who is the male counterpart of Sakti, are comparatively few in number. The bulk of them are found in the Surmā Valley. Another small sect remarkable for the peculiarity of its tenets is the Sahaj Bhajan. Each worshipper endeavours to secure salvation by taking a woman as a spiritual guide, but it is said that at their midnight meetings there is much sexual license under the cloak of religion. It is, however, possible that these charges are merely the calumnies with which a new creed is usually assailed by the supporters of the established order.

The standard form of Hindu temple is a domeshaped structure enclosing the shrine, approached by a short nave. It is usually built of thin flat bricks, with a fine glaze, and enriched with bas-reliefs; but there are comparatively few of these masonry buildings in the Province. Almost every village in Assam proper contains, however, a large barn-like structure, called the *namghor*, in which the people assemble for prayer and worship. In the Surmā Valley there are few temples or places of this kind, and the ordinary Hindu performs his devotions in a part of his house which is specially reserved for that purpose. Places of worship.

About one-fourth of the population of the Province, or 1,581,317 persons, returned themselves as Muhammadans in 1901. Nearly three-fourths of them were found in the District of Sylhet, which was conquered at the end of the 14th century by Sikandar Ghāzī, who was largely assisted in his enterprise by the famous Muhammadan fakīr Shāh Jalāl. This man was a native of Yemen in Arabia and was sent by his uncle to Hindustān with a handful of earth, and orders to settle in the place in which the earth was similar to the sample he took with him. The ground of Sylhet proved to be of the quality desired, and Shāh Jalāl settled in the newly-conquered territory. A fine mosque, which is thought to be of peculiar sanctity, has been built over his tomb, and a monthly grant is made by Government for its support. The tombs of the 360 disciples of the great fakīr are to be seen in almost every portion of the town. Muhammadans are also fairly numerous in Cāchār, which for many years has acted as an outlet for the surplus population of Sylhet, and in Goālpāra, where they form more than a quarter of the total population. The Assam Valley was invaded by the Muhammadans on several occasions, and one general is said to have penetrated as far as Sadiyā; but Goālpāra was the only District which they held for any length of time, and the influences of the faith were not largely felt at the eastern end of the valley. In the hills less than three per cent. of the population professed Islām, the majority of whom were working on the railway in North Cāchār, or living in the tarai Muhammadanism.

at the foot of the Gāro Hills. Only 2,724 persons wer returned as Shiahs, and 47 as members of the strict reformir sect known as Ahl-i-hadis, or Wahābis. The remainder, so f as they returned any sect at all, were Sunnis. The Moriās a small sect of degraded Muhammadans, who are said to be descend from the followers of Turbak, a Pathān who invaded Assam in th 16th century, and was there defeated and killed. They were employed by their captors in various capacities, for which they showed themselves to be totally unfitted, and were ultimately made braziers. They are looked down upon by their neighbours, and the number of persons who admit that they are Moriās naturally does not tend to increase. Muhammadan mosques are usually small brick structures, and consist of an open quadrangle with a covered arcade at the west end, but in some of the remoter parts of the Province service is held in a thatched hut.

Animism, etc. No less than 1,068,334 persons, or 17 per cent. of the population, still profess those various forms of primitive belief, which are usually described as animistic. The main feature of this religion is the desire to propitiate the devils who are ever on the alert to injure man, though most tribes recognise the existence of kindly spirits and the possibility of a future life. The number of unconverted tribesmen living in the Surmā Valley is very small, but in the four lower Districts of the valley of the Brahmaputra the proportion varies from 31 per cent. in Nowgong to 21 per cent. in Kāmrūp. In Sibsāgar the animistic tribes are only 7 per cent., and in Lakhimpur 5 per cent. of the total population. In the hill Districts they form 85 per cent. of the whole. The tribesmen have no special preference for their own forms of religion, and attorn fairly readily to Hinduism in the plains, and to Christianity in the hills. Conversion would, in fact, proceed rapidly, were it not for the natural reluctance of these primitive people to abandon pork, liquor, and the freedom of intercourse between the sexes permitted by their own religion. Apart from Christianity, the only other religions requiring mention are those of the Buddhists (8,911), the majority of whom are found in Lakhimpur and Sibsāgar, and Jains (1,797), who are usually merchants from Ajmer-Merwāra.

Christianity. The total number of Christians in Assam in 1901 was, Europeans and allied races 2,099, Eurasians 275, natives 33,595. Between 1891 and 1901 the number of native Christians increased by 128 per cent. The chief proselytizing agency in the Province is the Welsh Presbyterian Mission, whose headquarters are in the Khāsi and Jaintiā Hills. This mission was started in 1841, and in 1903 gave employment to 36 missionaries, of whom 13 were stationed in the Surmā Valley and 2 in the Lushai Hills. There is no caste system or social prejudice among the Khāsis to act as an obstacle to conversion; they come but little under the influence of Hinduism, and their readiness to accept the Christian faith can be judged from the fact that in 1901 nearly 9 per cent. of the population of the District returned themselves under this head. The Baptist Mission has also met with a large measure of success, the numbers of this sect having risen from 3,767 in 1891 to 10,045 at the last census. The mission was first started at Sadiyá in the Lakhimpur District in 1836, and in 1903 had 21 missionaries. Their main centres are in the Gáro Hills, Goálpára, Kāmrūp, and Sibsāgar Districts. Both the Anglican and Roman Catholic Churches are included in the Diocese of Calcutta.

The number of persons in British territory returned under the main religions at the last two enumerations is shown below :—

Religions.		1891.	1901.
Hindus ...		2,997,072	3,258,522
Animists ...		928,175	965,027
Musalmāns		1,483,974	1,570,934
Christians	Native ...	14,762	33,587
	Others ...	2,082	2,337
Buddhists		7,697	8,766
Others ...		1,481	2,705

The economic organization of the Province is of a very simple character, and the great mass of the population are supported by agriculture. In the hills and the Assam Valley there is very little subdivision of function, and the ordinary cultivator builds and repairs his own houses, makes his own agricultural implements, has his clothes woven at home, and in fact supplies almost all his own simple wants. The occupations returned in 1901 were divided into eight main classes. The number of persons supported by each class and the percentage they form of the total population were as follows:—Government 34,791, or ·6 per cent.; pasture and agriculture 5,172,228, or 84·5 per cent.; personal services 75,395, or 1·2 per cent.; preparation and supply of material substances 479,358, or 7·8 per cent.; commerce, transport, and storage 86,497, or 1·4 per cent.; professions 84,971, or 1·4 per cent.; unskilled labour other than agricultural 111,401, or 1·8 per cent.; means of subsistence

Occupation.

independent of occupation 81,702, or 1·3 per cent. The number of actual workers was almost exactly equal to the number of persons who were supported by others. Of the total number of workers, 1,073,776, or 35 per cent., were women, the great majority of whom took an active share in the cultivation of the land, for, though a woman may not touch the plough, she is very frequently employed to transplant paddy seedlings or reap the crop when ripe.

Food and dress.

The staple food of the people is boiled rice, eaten with pulse, spices, and fish or vegetable curry. Among the well-to-do, pigeon or duck occasionally take the place of fish, but fish is a very common article of diet in the plains, and is said to be a substitute for *ghī*, which is not very largely used. Goat's flesh is eaten by Muhammadans and Hindus alike, while venison is always acceptable, and in parts of the Assam Valley by no means rare. The restrictions on the eating of flesh are not so stringent as in upper India, and even respectable Brāhmans take duck, pigeon, and goat. Fowls like beef are debarred to the Hindu, and so are sheep, though in parts of Sylhet ram's flesh is eaten even by the higher castes. An orthodox Brāhman in that District will only take food once between sunrise and sunset, but this rule is not observed in the Assam Valley. Domesticated pork is of course forbidden to both Hindu and Muhammadan, but the lower Hindu castes will sometimes eat wild pig. Tea drinking is very common, especially in the early morning. Sweetmeats usually consist of powdered grain mixed with milk, sugar, and *ghī*. The hill men and the aboriginal tribes eat flesh of all kinds, even when nearly putrid. Dog is generally considered a luxury by them, and lizards, snakes, and insects are appreciated, but milk is very seldom taken. The ordinary form of dress for a villager is a cotton *dhoti* or waistcloth, with a big shawl or wrapper, and sometimes a cotton coat or waistcoat. Women in Assam wear a petticoat, a scarf tied round the bust, and a shawl. In the Assam Valley these clothes are generally home made, and in the case of the women, and of the large wraps used in the cold weather by men, are frequently of silk. A curious article of dress is a large flat hat, called *jhapi*, which serves as a protection against the sun and rain, and is made of leaves and split bamboo and decorated with coloured cloth. These hats are circular in shape, and range from 2 to 4 feet in diameter, but those of the larger size are more often carried than worn. In the Surmā Valley women wear a *sārī*, a piece of cloth about 15 feet long and nearly 4 feet broad; this is fastened round the waist to form a petticoat, and then brought over the head and shoulders so as to cover the rest of the body. Chemises and bodices are also sometimes used. In this part of the Province there is very little home-made cloth. Manchester piece-goods are in great request and machine-made coats and shirts are largely worn. The dress of the middle classes does not differ materially from that of the ordinary villager, but a superior material is employed, and shirts are usually worn. In the Assam Valley beautiful silk and cotton cloths are woven by the wives and daughters of the well-to-do, and fine embroidered cloths are produced in Manipur. Boots and shoes are the exception, and in their own homes even the richer people wear wooden clogs. Wooden sandals are also used by villagers in the Assam Valley when travelling or working in jungle ground, where there are tufts of sharp-pointed grass. In the hills several fashions are in vogue. Beyond the frontier, some of the Nāgā tribes go absolutely naked, and even in British territory both men and women are often content with the very minimum of apparel. The state dress of the Khāsis, on the other hand, consists of a silk waistcloth and richly-embroidered tunic, set off with much handsome jewellery, and an Angāmī Nāgā in his war-paint is a distinctly impressive sight.

Dwellings

The house of the ordinary villager consists of three or four small and ill-ventilated rooms, built round three sides of a court-yard. The walls are usually made of reeds plastered over with mud, the roof of thatch supported on bamboos, the floor of mud. In the Assam Valley the materials required for the construction of a house do not, as a rule, cost the proprietor anything but the labour of procuring them, but the houses are small and generally badly built. In the Surmā Valley the villagers take more trouble, the cottages are raised on high plinths, are well thatched, and have an arched roof tree to resist the storms. Brick houses are very rare, and the dwellings of the middle class are in the same style, but larger and of better quality, than the cottage of the villager. The furniture of the cultivating classes is simple, and consists of a few boxes and wicker-work stools, brass and bell-metal cooking utensils, earthen pots and pans, baskets, and bottles, and in the Assam Valley a loom. The villager sometimes sleeps on a small bamboo *machan* or platform, and sometimes on a mat on the floor, but the middle classes have beds, tables, and chairs in their houses. The animistic tribes usually build on piles, the floor being raised a few feet above the ground. The house consists of one long building divided into cubicles by a few partitions. Among certain tribes this building is enlarged to meet the wants of the growing family, and sometimes as many as 60 souls reside in one long barrack.

Disposal dead.

Hindus burn and Muhammadans bury their dead. Some animistic tribes follow the Hindu custom, unless the death has been due to an infectious disease, when they are afraid of the infection being carried in the smoke of the funeral pyre; others bury, while a few tribes simply throw dead bodies into the jungle. Some tribes preserve the corpses of their wealthier men for several months after their death. They are placed in wooden coffins inside the house, and the liquid matter is carried off through a bamboo. The Paithes, who live in the Lushai Hills, smear a greasy preparation over the body, which preserves and hardens the skin. The corpse is then dressed in its best clothes, and in the evening is brought outside the house, and rice beer is poured down its throat. This disgusting performance is sometimes continued for several weeks.

Amusements. Dice, cards, and chess are played by the well-to-do, and the cultivators in the Assam Valley amuse themselves with simple theatrical performances, music, singing, dancing, buffalo and cock fights, and in places with a game in which two eggs are banged together, a forfeit being paid for the one that is broken. The ordinary Hindu festivals, such as the Holī, Rath Jātra, Janmāshtami, Kālī and Durgā pūjās are observed. Special celebrations are the Bishori pūjā in honour of the goddess of snakes and the Kārtik pūjā in Sylhet, and the Māgh and Baisākh Bihus in Assam. The Māgh Bihu is the harvest home. The cultivators feast after having gathered in their crops, bathe at dawn, and then warm themselves at bonfires of rice straw, which have been prepared several weeks beforehand, and which form quite a conspicuous feature in the rural landscape towards the end of December. The Baisākh Bihu, which ushers in the new year, lasts for a week, and is an occasion of some license. Boys and girls join in songs and dances of a somewhat unrestrained character, and lapses from chastity are considered almost venial. This festival not unfrequently gives rise to suits for abduction against lovers who have induced the object of their affections to elope with them, instead of paying the usual bride price to the parents of the girl. The anniversaries of the deaths of the two Vaishnavite reformers, Sankar Deb and Mādhab Deb, are also observed by the Assamese. In the Surmā Valley the villagers indulge in boat-races in long canoes, manned by from fifteen to twenty pairs of paddlers, who keep time to the songs of a man who dances in the centre of the vessel, and beats a pair of cymbals. The Khāsis are much addicted to archery competitions, and are very skilful with the bow, and the Nāgās amuse themselves by putting the weight, leaping, and exercises on the horizontal bar.

The best-known game of all is, however, polo, which is supposed by some to have been introduced to European players from Manipur, and which is still played by the natives of that State with the greatest enthusiasm. A good Manipuri pony, though seldom over 12 hands high, has, for its size, remarkable speed, courage, and endurance. There are usually from five to seven players on each side, there are often no goal posts, and no attention is paid to the rules prohibiting crossing, fouling, or reckless use of the stick. The rush of a Manipurī team thus suggests a cavalry regiment practising shock tactics, and were it not for the small size of the ponies serious accidents would frequently occur. The pony's bridle is covered with large brightly-coloured balls of wool, the rider's legs are protected by curious leather shields, and while the upper part of his body is clothed in gay attire, and his calves covered with gaiters, his thighs are almost naked. The general effect is most striking. The men possess a wonderful command over the ball, and hit it from almost any position in any direction.

Names and titles.

Hindus of the higher castes usually have two names, one corresponding to the Christian name of Europe, the other a family name. The number of family names is, however, so small that they do not give much clue to the individuality of the bearer. A caste name such as Sarmā for Brāhmans, Gupta for Baidyas, and Das for all castes other than these two is sometimes added. Titles such as Rai, Chowdhury, Mazumdar, Gohain, Phukan, Baruah, are, however, in common use, especially in the Assam Valley. Proper names are often of a grandiloquent character, such as "Lord of the earth and moon," "Delight of women"; but children are sometimes called after the day of the week or the month in which they were born. Women usually bear the names of goddesses or flowers. Among the poorer people names like Fedela, "The dirty one," are sometimes given with the idea of averting the jealousy of the gods. The Khāsis attach the male prefix U and the female prefix Ka to all proper names. Common affixes of place names are "*ganj*" in the Surmā Valley, which indicates a market, "*pur*," a town, and in Assam "*garh*," a fort and embankment, "*gao*," a village, "*dai*," water and "*ranga*," red, referring to the colour of the soil.

AGRICULTURE.

Character of soil and system of cultivation.

The Province of Assam consists, as has been already mentioned, of two great alluvial plains, surrounded on three sides by mountains. The soil formation thus falls into two main classes, that of the hill tracts, which are being denuded, and that of the valleys, which are being formed by the same process. There is a further difference between the conditions prevailing in the two valleys, due to the difference in their elevation above sea level. During the rainy season there is usually a strong current in the Brahmaputra and the other rivers of the Assam Valley, and where the current is swift it is only the heavier portion of the matter held in suspension—that is, the sand—which is deposited. In the Surmā Valley, where there is very little fall, the rivers are sluggish, and when they overflow enrich the fields with silt. Silt is also deposited in the Assam Valley in slack water away from the main current, and the soil of that Division consists of a mixture of clay and sand in varying proportions, which ranges from pure sand to clay so stiff as to be hardly fit for cultivation.

The land best adapted for the growth of rice, the staple food crop of the Province, is a deep, soft, clayey loam, which has been rendered light and friable by the action of worms. When there is too much sand the soil is too light to retain the water, which is necessary for the development of the crop. Where the clay is too stiff, it is impervious to air and water, and difficult to plough, and the roots of the plant are likely to be choked. The fertility of the soil is also largely affected by the quantity of organic matter it contains. This humus, or vegetable mould, is formed by the decomposition of vegetable matter, and is most abundant in land that has long remained under jungle. It contains nitrogen, which is one of the most important elements of plant food, and is useful alike to clayey and sandy soils. The former it renders less clinging and less liable to bake into hard clods, while to the latter it gives more adhesion and greater capacity to retain water. A further advantage is to be found in its solvent action on the iron in the earth. By this means it tends to check the formation of the hard red pan, which often underlies thin poor soils, and injures the crop by interfering with the growth of the roots. The suitability of land for rice, depends, however, chiefly upon its elevation, and its capacity for retaining moisture.

The Brahmaputra Valley.

Generally speaking, the country on either side of the Brahmaputra falls into four broad classes. The first is the *chapari*, or land in the immediate neighbourhood of the river, which is heavily flooded in the rains. It is, as a rule, covered with high grass jungle, which has to be cut down and burned before it can be brought under cultivation, but, when the floods do not rise too soon, it yields excellent crops of *ahu*, or summer rice. The seed is sown in March or April and reaped in June or July, and is followed by a crop of mustard or pulse, which is sown when the river falls in October and November, and gathered about three months later. When the land is first cleared of jungle it is free from weeds, but they spring up with great rapidity in the second and third year of cropping, and it is then abandoned for from eight to ten years to allow the high jungle time to kill them out. Behind the *chaparis* comes a belt of low-lying land, in which *bao*, a long-stemmed variety of rice, is grown. It is usually sown in April or May and reaped in November and December. Summer rice is sometimes mixed with *bao* in the hope of getting a crop before the river rises. The water drains off slowly from this belt, and the land is left too cold and damp for winter crops. The level of the country then gradually rises above the reach of ordinary floods, and *sali*, or transplanted winter rice, becomes the staple crop. The grain is sown in nursery beds, the seedlings are transplanted in June or July, when they are about two months old, and the harvest is reaped in November and December. *Sali* is divided into two main varieties, *bar* and *lahi*. The former gives a heavier yield, but ripens later and requires more water than *lahi*, and is therefore usually planted on lower land. This belt of land is a broad one, and contains most of the permanent cultivation and the bulk of the agricultural population. Beyond this again comes the submontane tract. The level of the land is higher, and the fields are often irrigated from the hill streams. The chief crop is *sali*, or a transplanted form of *ahu* known as *kharma*. This land is practically free from all risk of flood, and artificial irrigation renders the harvest particularly secure.

These four belts are not, however, found in all parts of the valley. Very little *bao* is grown in the Districts of Darrang, Sibsāgar, and Lakhimpur, and though, as a rule, there are *chaparis* on both sides of the Brahmaputra, there are places where the margin of permanent cultivation comes almost down to the river bank. Sugarcane is usually planted on high land near the village site in the broad belt of permanent cultivation.

The Surma Valley. The conditions of the Surmā Valley are somewhat different. There are no *chaparis*, and the banks of the rivers are the highest and the most fertile part. In Cāchār and the eastern part of Sylhet the bulk of the land resembles that found in the broad belt of permanent cultivation in Assam, and the staple crops are *sail* and *aus*, which correspond to the *sali* and *ahu* of the other valley. The western portion of Sylhet becomes one great swamp in the rains, and is only fit for the cultivation of *aman*, a form of long-stemmed paddy. A fourth kind of rice called *sailbura* is grown in the large *haors* or basins to which reference has been already made. It is sown at the end of the rains and harvested about May, and gives an exceptionally large yield per acre. Sugarcane is often grown on low land, and mustard on old high land near the village site, where it not unnaturally gives a poorer outturn than that of the fertile river banks of Assam.

The hill Districts. The majority of the hill tribes cultivate on the *jhūm* system. A patch of land is cleared with axe and fire, the soil is hoed up, and the seeds of hill rice, chillies, cotton, millets, gourds, and other vegetables dibbled in among the ashes. The same plot is seldom cropped for more than two or three years in succession. After this time the weeds spring up in great luxuriance, and further cultivation would destroy the roots of *ikra* or bamboo jungle, upon the growth of which the land depends for its fertility. *Jhūms* are left fallow for as long a time as possible. The shortest period is four years, but it is generally extended to eight or ten. In the Khāsi Hills rice is grown in terraced and well-irrigated fields in the valleys, but other crops, such as potatoes and millet, are raised on the bare hill side. The Tankul and Angāmi country lies too high for the successful cultivation of *jhūm* rice, and there is not sufficient land to permit the people to rely entirely on this system of cultivation.

The villages of these tribes are surrounded by admirably constructed terraced rice fields built up with stone retaining walls at different levels, and irrigated by skilfully designed channels, which distribute the water over each step in the series.

Method of cultivation.

The agricultural implements are all of a very primitive character, and include a wooden plough with an iron-tipped share, wooden rakes and mallets, a rough bamboo harrow, sickles, bill-hooks, knives, and baskets. In Assam proper sugarcane is pressed between two grooved logs of wood, turned by a pole, and the iron mill, though more expeditious and economical, is little used. Winter rice is sown in carefully-manured beds near the homestead, which at the commencement of the rains form brilliant patches of green in the landscape. While the shoots are growing, the cultivator ploughs his fields some four or five times, reducing the soil to a fine puddle of clay and repairs the low mounds intended to retain the water. In Assam proper the seedlings are planted out in handfuls by the women, who can be seen up to their knees in mud, stooping for hours together under the burning summer sun. The distance at which the clumps are placed depends upon the quality of the soil, and varies from eight inches to three feet. As the crop grows, it covers the plain with a rich carpet of green, turning towards the end of the year to a fine yellow. When ripe, the grain is cut off near the head, tied in bundles, and carried, slung from bamboos, to the homestead, where it is threshed out by cattle as occasion requires. *Bao* or *aman* and *ahu* are sown broadcast, but the yield is usually smaller, and the quality of the grain is not so fine. Mustard requires four or five ploughings, and when new land is broken up the cultivators have to press down the high grass jungle and wait till it is sufficiently withered to catch fire. Sugarcane is a crop which, though yielding good returns, entails a considerable amount of labour. The land is generally ploughed twice for pulse, but the seed is sometimes sown broadcast over fields that have just yielded a crop of rice. The plants are pulled up when ripe, left to dry for a week or ten days, and brought in at the leisure of the cultivator.

Assam is a purely rural country, with no large towns, and in 1901 no less than 84 per cent. of the population returned agriculture as their means of livelihood. The proportion of agriculturists in the different Districts was highest in the Gáro, Nágá, and Lushai Hills, and in Darrang, Nowgong, and Sibsāgar. It was lowest in Kámrūp and Sylhet, where there were large numbers of fishermen and priests.

Area under different crops.

The area under different crops in the five upper Districts of the Brahmaputra valley is returned by the local revenue officials. The figures may be accepted as fairly accurate, but do not, as a rule, include the comparatively small area occupied by tribes not assessed to land revenue. The principal crops raised are rice, pulse, tea, sugarcane, and rape and mustard. The area under these crops will be found in table IV appended to this article, but this table gives a very imperfect idea of the cultivated area of the Province, as it does not include the hill Districts, Sylhet and Goálpára, for the greater part of which there are no returns, or Cāchār, the figures for which have only become available of recent years. As a matter of fact, there are probably at least four million acres under rice in Assam, and well over a quarter of a million under mustard.

Wheat is sown in Goálpára, where it is believed that there are about 10,000 acres under this crop; elsewhere both wheat and barley are only raised in small patches by foreigners. Jute is grown on a commercial scale in Goálpára and Sylhet, and is gradually extending into Kámrūp, but in the rest of the Province the villagers only plant enough to supply the home demand. The estimated area under jute in 1903-04 was 39,000 acres. Linseed is largely grown in Sylhet, but is not common elsewhere. Garden crops include tobacco, several kinds of plantain, vegetables, *pān*, the areca-nut, pepper, and various kinds of spices. In the Surmā Valley *pān* is grown in the orthodox way by Baruis in neatly-fenced gardens, completely covered with the tendrils of the plant, but in Assam it is usually trained up the stem of the areca-nut tree. Plantains of different kinds are found near every house, and in the Assam Valley the ash is largely used as a substitute for salt, the people still clinging to the customs which prevailed in the days of native rule, when mineral salt could not be easily obtained. Pepper is mentioned in Welsh's Report on Assam, in 1794, as a plant that throve well, but, though the cultivation would be most lucrative, only a small quantity is grown. The Khāsis export potatoes, oranges, pineapples, and the leaves of the bay tree, and cotton is grown by most of the hill tribes. It has a very short and somewhat harsh staple, but it is useful to mix with wool and the proportion of seed is unusually low.

In Cāchār the rice crop is usually distributed under the three chief varieties of the grain in the following proportions: *sail* or *sali* 70 per cent., *aus* or *ahu* 22 per cent., *aman* or *bao* 8 per cent. For the Assam Valley the proportion is *sali* 70 per cent., *ahu* 22 per cent., and *bao* 8 per cent. *Ahu* and *bao* are chiefly grown in lower Assam; in Darrang, Sibságar, and Lakhimpur there is not much *ahu* and hardly any *bao*. The normal yield of *sali* rice is about 9 cwt. of cleaned grain per acre, and that of *ahu* and *bao* about a cwt. less. Mustard gives about 5 cwt. of seed, and sugarcane about a ton of raw molasses per acre. These figures only represent a rough general standard; the actual crop obtained is often considerably in excess or defect of this mean.

Cowdung and the sweepings of the courtyard are used to manure garden crops, sugarcane, jute, and the nurseries in which rice seedlings Use of manure.

are grown, and in the more congested parts of the Province cowdung is sometimes spread on the rice fields themselves. The *chaparis* and shifting cultivation of the hill tribes are enriched by the ashes of the jungle with which the land was originally covered. Exhausted tea land is top-dressed with richer soil, and on some gardens the use of oilcake and farm-yard manure is coming into favour. The Khāsis fully appreciate the value of cowdung as a fertilizer, but all over the Province immense quantities of this excellent manure are allowed to go to waste. There is practically no rotation of crops, apart from the system under which summer rice is followed by pulse or mustard, while pulse is usually sown on the rice-seedling bed, as it is thought to benefit the soil.

Extension of cultivation.

It is impossible to obtain accurate figures showing the extension of cultivation in the Province as a whole. No statistics are available for the hills, or the permanently settled estates of Sylhet and Goálpára, and there is a considerable difference between the conditions prevailing in the two valleys. In Assam proper and in the Eastern Duārs the extension of cultivation is best measured by the growth of the area settled at full rates, excluding the land held by planters. The area so settled in 1881-82 was 1,335,000 acres. During the next ten years there was an increase of 15 per cent., which was, however, partly due to the operations of the cadastral party, and to greater strictness in the measurement of land. Then ensued a period of extreme depression in lower and central Assam, and by 1902-1903 the area settled in this way had only increased by 63,000 acres, or 4 per cent. more than the total for 1891-92. This slow rate of increase in a Division where there are enormous tracts of culturable waste land available for settlement, was due to exceptional mortality which seriously reduced the indigenous population, and to the damage done by the earthquake of 1897, which interfered with the natural drainage in lower Assam.

The settled area of Cāchār has increased rapidly since it came under British rule. In 1843, when the first settlement was made, the area covered by the operations was only 97,900 acres. In 1903 the settled area of the District was 607,000 acres. The cultivated area held on ordinary tenure increased by 24 per cent. between 1883-84 and 1896-97. It is impossible to ascertain the extent to which cultivation has extended in the Sylhet District as a whole, but in the Jaintiā Parganas the cropped area increased by 22 per cent. during the currency of the last settlement, which was for a period of 15 years. The great obstacle to the extension of cultivation is the absence of a labouring class. In the Surmā Valley, Kámrūp, and Goālpāra agricultural labourers are extremely scarce, and in central and upper Assam they are practically non-existent. The climate of the country in the rains is not calculated to stimulate the inhabitants to prolonged physical exertion, and ryots, who are compelled to plough, plant, and reap with their own hands, are not likely to cultivate more land than is absolutely necessary for their maintenance.

The villagers usually select the best heads of rice for seed grain, but are not very prompt to adopt new varieties. The cultivation of jute on the commercial scale is slowly spreading up the Assam Valley, and the *ras* and *balam* varieties of rice have recently been tried. Potatoes were introduced into the Khāsi Hills by Mr. Scott in 1830, and are now extensively cultivated in that District. Of recent years the plants have been attacked by disease, but fresh varieties have been imported by Government, and have been much appreciated by the villagers. An experimental farm is maintained near Shillong, and scientific farming has been undertaken on a small scale by Europeans and Bengalis in Darrang. Efforts have been made by the Agricultural department from time to time to introduce new and improved varieties of seed, but the results produced have been inconsiderable. In 1903, a garden of European fruit trees was opened near Shillong, as the Khāsis can be relied upon to adopt without delay any forms of fruit culture that seem likely to prove remunerative. Introduction of new varieties.

Generally speaking, there is not much serious indebtedness among the cultivators of the Province, and the creditors themselves are often agriculturists. In Assam there is no rich upper or middle class, and few natives other than the Márwāris are possessed of any capital. The rate of interest is in consequence extremely high, and varies from 37½ to 75 per cent. per annum. In parts of the Assam Valley it is the custom for the poorer villagers to take advances from traders on the standing crop, which is subsequently sold at a price below that ruling in the open market. This is especially the case with mustard, which cannot always be removed till the rivers rise in the rains. In the Surmā Valley the producer often deals direct with the trader from Bengal, and the practice of giving advances is not so common. In Sylhet it is said that the indebtedness of the cultivators is increasing. New wants have arisen, but the villagers do not care to make the additional exertions required to provide the means to gratify them. Wages, however, still run high, so that there cannot be much in the shape of poverty, and it is seldom necessary for Government to make loans to agriculturists. The total amount so distributed in 1903-04 was less than Rs. 24,000. Agricultural loans.

The cattle of Assam are a peculiarly degenerate breed. The causes of their degeneracy are not altogether clear, but it is probably largely due to a complete disregard of all the laws of breeding, to overwork, and absolute neglect. The valley of the Brahmaputra is exceptionally well supplied with grazing grounds, and there are few places even in the more densely-settled tracts where pasture land cannot be obtained within five miles of the village site. The Cattle, ponies and sheep.

grazing near the village is, however, usually poor, and far inferior to the rich grass that grows in the cold weather on the marshes that fringe the banks of the Brahmaputra and its tributaries. Where grazing is not readily obtainable, paddy straw is used as fodder. In the Surmā Valley the *haors*, or great depressions, to which reference has been already made, afford excellent grazing in the cold weather, but in the rains the cattle are almost entirely stall-fed on straw, or grass dragged from the bottom of the flooded tracts. The villagers pay very little attention to the comfort of their animals, and their condition is not much better than that of the cattle in Assam proper. In the hills the cattle, though small, are fat and sturdy, and, where milked, give a small but very rich supply. The buffaloes in the valley of the Brahmaputra are particularly fine animals, but they have been largely supplemented by the smaller breed imported from Bengal. There is no indigenous breed of sheep, or, except in Manipur, of ponies. The Manipurī pony is a very hardy little animal, but unfortunately the breed has nearly died out. Cart bullocks are imported from northern India, and ponies and sheep from Bhután. The average price of farm stock is :—buffalo Rs. 50 to Rs. 70, plough bullock Rs. 15 to Rs. 25, cow Rs. 8 to Rs. 15, and goat Rs. 2-8 to Rs. 4. Serious loss is caused by rinderpest, foot-and-mouth disease, diarrhœa and dysentery, and other forms of cattle disease. There is only one Veterinary Surgeon in the Province, who has been entertained by the local boards of the Sibságar District.

Irrigation and flood protection.

No irrigation works have been constructed by Government, and no distinction has hitherto been drawn by the Agricultural department or the Settlement Officer between irrigated and unirrigated land. Irrigation is, however, freely resorted to by the Kachóris and Meches, who live near the foot of the Himālayas in the Assam Valley. The villagers combine together and construct small channels, sometimes of considerable length, through which they convey the water of the hill streams to their fields. The abundance and certainty of the crop fully repay them for the labour expended on the work. In Sylhet the water in the cold weather is dammed up in the lowest part of the *haors* and thence diverted on to the *boro* rice crop. Mention has already been made of the irrigation works of the Khāsīs and Angāmī Nágás. In normal years, however, the rainfall in every part of the Province is so abundant that the crops seldom suffer from want of moisture, and the chief danger to cultivation arises from flood. The system of forced labour which prevailed under the Ahom Rájás enabled them to construct embankments along the Brahmaputra and many of its tributaries, some of which are still kept in repair. These works were especially numerous in the Sibsāgar District in the neighbourhood of the Rájá's capital, and the country was protected from the floods of the

Brahmaputra, the Disāng, the Dikho, the Dihing, and the Dariká. A considerable sum of money has already been expended by the British Government on the maintenance of these embankments, and a scheme is under consideration for the reclamation of a large area which is now exposed to flood. Raised roads along the banks of rivers are also common in lower Assam.

From the commercial point of view tea is the most important crop raised in Assam. The first discovery of the tea-plant growing wild in upper Assam, in 1821, is generally assigned to Mr. Robert Bruce, who had proceeded thither on a mercantile exploration. The country then formed part of the Burmese dominions. But the first Burmese war shortly afterwards broke out, and a brother of the first discoverer having been appointed in 1826 to the command of a flotilla of gunboats, followed up the subject, and obtained several hundred plants and a quantity of seed. Some specimens were ultimately forwarded to the Superintendent of the Botanic Gardens at Calcutta. In 1832, Captain Jenkins was deputed by the Governor-General of India, Lord William Bentinck, to report upon the resources of Assam, and the tea-plant was specially brought to his notice by Mr. Bruce. In 1834, Lord William Bentinck recorded a minute, stating that his attention had been called to the subject previous to his having left England to take up the Governor-Generalship, and he appointed a committee to prosecute inquiries, and to promote the cultivation of the plant. Communications were opened with China with a view to obtain fresh plants and seeds, and a deputation, composed of gentlemen versed in botanical studies, was despatched to Assam. Seed was obtained from China; but it was ascertained that the tea-plant was indigenous in Assam, and might be multiplied to any extent. Another result of the Chinese mission, the procuring of persons skilled in the cultivation and manufacture of black tea, was of more material benefit. Subsequently, under Lord Auckland, a further supply of Chinese cultivators and manufacturers was obtained, men well acquainted with the processes necessary for the production of green tea, as the former set were with those requisite for black. The experimental introduction of tea-planting into Assam was undertaken by Government. In 1835, the first tea garden was opened at Lakhimpur. In 1838, the first twelve chests of tea from Assam were received in England. They had been injured in some degree on the passage; but on samples being submitted to brokers, the reports were highly favourable. It was, however, the intention of Government not to carry on the trade, but to resign it to private enterprise as soon as the experimental cultivation proved successful. Mercantile associations for the planting and manufacture of tea in Assam began to be formed in 1839; and in 1840 Government made over its experimental

The tea industry.

establishment to the Assam Tea Company. In 1851, the crop of this Company was estimated at 280,000 pounds. In 1854, gardens were opened in Darrang and Kámrūp; and in 1855 the plant was discovered growing wild in Cáchár. During the next ten years, capital flowed into the business from all quarters. Land was recklessly taken up, to be sold to speculators in England for extravagant sums; and tea-growing for a time fell into the hands of stockjobbers and bubble companies. The crash came in 1866; and for the next few years this promising industry lay in a condition of extreme depression.

Development in recent years.

About 1869, matters began to amend, and during the last thirty years there has been a great development of the industry. The returns for 1871 showed (in round figures) that 11 million pounds of tea were manufactured in the Province. For 1881 the figures were 37 million pounds; for 1891, 90 million pounds; and for 1900, 141 million pounds. The supply had by this time begun to show unmistakeable signs of exceeding the demand, and attempts were made to restrict the output by the introduction of a system of finer plucking. This was, however, but a temporary check and in 1903 the output exceeded 145 million pounds. There were in that year 764 gardens, which gave employment to 846 Europeans and 409,000 natives. The average outturn was 445 pounds per acre, and the crop was valued at wholesale prices in Calcutta at more than 3¼ million sterling. The capital invested in tea is probably about £ 30 for every acre under cultivation, and as 338,000 acres were planted out in 1903, the capital value of the gardens in Assam may be estimated at nearly ten and a quarter million sterling.* Some four-fifths of the capital employed by companies is owned by companies whose headquarter offices are situated in England.

The labour supply.

The want of labour has always been one of the most serious obstacles to the development of the industry. The mass of the population of the Province are above the necessity of working for wages, and nearly all the coolies employed on the plantations have to be imported from other parts of India. Assam is, however, unpopular among the labouring classes, the journey from the recruiting Districts is troublesome and expensive, the class of persons capable of working successfully in the damp climate of the Province is limited, and of recent years the supply of labour available has not been sufficient to satisfy the requirements of the planters. Special Acts have been passed to regulate the relations between the employers and their labour force. Careful provision is made for the welfare of the cooly. He is housed in neat and

* A considerable proportion of this tea property is held by private owners. The capital value of gardens owned by public companies appears to be about £ 40 per acre, and this estimate, if applied to the total acreage, shows a capital value of 13½ million sterling.

comfortable lines, he is provided with an excellent water-supply, generally drawn from masonry wells, and when sick he is cared for in a comfortable hospital by a native doctor working under the supervision of a European medical man. The provision of all these comforts and the importation of the labourers themselves cost large sums of money, which no one would be willing to expend without some guarantee that the coolies when imported would consent to remain on the plantation. This protection is afforded by the law, which lays down that a labourer, provided that he is well treated, must not leave the garden to which he is indentured before the expiry of his contract, unless he chooses to redeem it by a money payment. During the ten years ending with June 30th, 1903, 543,800 persons were brought up to the tea gardens.

Class of land required.

The land best suited for the plant in the Brahmaputra Valley is the virgin soil of the dense forests at the foot of the hills, where the climate is hot and moist. In the Surmā Valley the most productive gardens are those planted on the low ranges of hills in the south of the Sylhet District, or on reclaimed marsh land. The yield in the Surmā Valley is higher than in Assam proper, but the cost of production and the price obtained for the manufactured tea are alike lower. Indigenous seed gives the best results, and after this a hybrid of indigenous and Chīna. It is many years since China seed was planted out in new clearances, and considerable areas covered by this plant have been abandoned. The most important tea Districts and their area under the plant in 1903 were Sibsāgar 78,500 acres, Sylhet 73,500 acres, Lakhimpur 69,300 acres, and Cāchār 60,000 acres.

System of tea manufacture.

The following is a short account of the system of cultivation and manufacture usually followed. The seed is first allowed to germinate and is then sown in carefully-selected nursery beds. When the plants are about 12 inches high they are planted out at distances of from 4 feet to 5 feet apart. As the bush grows it is pruned, in order to remove decayed or injured wood, to encourage the production of new shoots, and to form as large a surface for the latter purpose as possible. The wild tea tree grows to as much as 50 feet in height, whereas a well-pruned bush is between 3 feet and 4 feet high. When the plant is about three years old it is fit for plucking. The usual practice is to pick off the top of each young shoot, removing either two or three leaves and the bud. The shoot then germinates again and the plant thus yields eleven or twelve "flushes," as they are called, during the season.

When the leaf has been taken to the tea-house it is spread out in thin layers and allowed to wither, and then placed in the rolling machines. The object of rolling is to break up the cellular matter and liberate the juices, and to give a twist to the leaf. After the leaf has been rolled, it is spread out in a cool room to allow of oxidation taking place. As soon as this process is complete, it is placed in the firing machines until the last trace of moisture has been expelled, and the tea is crisp to the touch. It is then sifted, sorted, fired again, and finally packed in lead-lined boxes while it is still warm.

RENTS, WAGES, AND PRICES.

Rents.

In most of the Districts of Assam the actual cultivator of the soil usually holds direct from the state, and the area of land on which rent is paid is inconsiderable. A large part of Goálpára and of the more densely populated portions of Sylhet were, however, included in the permanent settlement of Bengal; and the system of land tenure in Cáchár, and the existence of large estates on privileged rates of revenue in Kámrūp, have tended to produce a tenant class, which at the last census amounted to more than one-third of the total number of persons supported by agriculture. The amount of waste land still available in the Province is, however, so enormous, that there is little risk of landlords exacting too large a proportion of the profits of the soil, and Sylhet and Goálpára are the only two Districts in which a tenancy law (Bengal Act VIII of 1869) is in force. In Sylhet, the rents charged vary from Rs. 12 to As. 12 for an acre of rice land, but the ordinary rate is about Rs. 3 an acre. There is a certain amount of competition among the cultivators to obtain land, but if the owner takes advantage of their necessities to raise the rates to an unreasonable pitch, he experiences great difficulty in realizing the demand. In Goálpára, which is very sparsely peopled, the rents vary from Rs. 6 to As. 12 an acre, the average rent paid by the cultivators for an acre of rice land being between two and three rupees. In Assam proper, there is very little sub-letting, except in Kámrūp. The rent usually charged is the amount assessed by Government at full rates on land of a similar class, but occasionally is as much as Rs. 6 for an acre of good rice land. In upper Assam rents of Rs. 9 an acre are sometimes paid for rice fields which are exceptionally fertile, or have some special advantages of site, but the total area sublet is small, and in a large number of cases the tenant merely pays the Government revenue assessed upon the holding. In Cáchár the average rent is about Rs. 6 per acre, and varies from Rs. 4-8 to Rs. 7-8.

Produce rents.

In place of cash rent the landlord occasionally receives a portion of the produce. In Sylhet the amount demanded is usually 3¼ cwt. of unhusked paddy per acre, but tenants prefer, as a rule, to pay in cash. In Assam the standard form of produce rent is the *adhi*, or half-share system. The owner of the land usually gives half the seed and pays the revenue; the tenant, as a rule, does the actual cultivation, but the crop can be divided at any stage, according to the terms of the agreement. The tenant's responsibilities sometimes cease when the land has been reduced to puddle, and the landlord has to transplant his seedlings and reap, carry, and thresh his share of the crop. At the other extreme come the cases where the tenant is required to thresh the grain before it is divided.

Over the greater part of the Province, the supply of local labour is extremely limited, and, although in most Districts the wages of unskilled labour are said to be six annas a day, it would be impossible to procure any considerable body of persons either for this or for a larger sum. Hired labour is not much used for cultivation, but when a labourer is employed he receives from four to five annas a day, grain being often given in lieu of cash. In lower Assam it is usually the practice to give a servant a large advance, which is gradually worked off; but in some cases the work done is set against the interest of the loan, so that the debt itself is never liquidated, and the debtor never succeeds in freeing himself from his obligations. It is, however, to the interest of the employer to treat his servants well, as he has little hope of recovering the loan if they choose to leave him; and they are generally well fed and clothed, and treated almost as members of the family. In Sylhet, the prejudice against working for hire is not so strong as in Assam proper, where the feeling appears to be partly due to a revulsion from the system of forced labour which prevailed under the Ahom Rájás. The ordinary wage paid to farm labourers is four annas a day, but at harvest time they often receive double that sum. Assam, however, practically depends for its labour supply upon other parts of India. Railways are built, roads are made, and gardens are worked by imported coolies. Male coolies on gardens usually earn from four to five rupees per mensem, and women about a rupee less, but they receive in addition substantial concessions in the shape of houses, water-supply, and medical comforts. Artisans are usually foreigners, and are said to earn from Rs. 15 to Rs. 30 per mensem. **Wages.**

Prices in Assam are still liable to strongly marked fluctuations and vary considerably in different parts of the Province. As a rule, they range high in upper Assam, where there is a large foreign population to be fed, and are fairly low in lower Assam and Sylhet. Since 1893, there has been a general tendency towards a rise, due partly to bad harvests in the Province, partly to famine in other parts of India, and partly to a large increase in the foreign population. In good seasons, however, rice is still by no means dear. In 1899 and 1900 the average price for the Province was nearly 15 seers for a rupee (=about 45 lb. for 2 shillings), as compared with an average for the six years ending with 1879 of 13½ seers (=about 40½ lb. for 2 shillings). Such extensions of cultivation as have taken place have not tended to reduce the price of rice, as their effect is more than counterbalanced by the increase in the foreign **Prices.**

population. The same cause has, to a great extent, nullified the effect produced by the improvement of communications, though in 1900, when there was a bad harvest in Cáchár, the stringency was relieved by the importation of large stocks of grain by the Assam-Bengal Railway. Generally speaking, the chief characteristic of Assam is sharp variations from year to year and also from place to place, a distance of a few miles being sometimes enough to double the price of grain. The average number of seers of rice to be purchased for a rupee during the five years ending with 1901 were Sylhet 13 (=about 39 lb. for 2 shillings), Kámrūp 12 (=about 36 lb. for 2 shillings), and Lakhimpur 10½ (=about 31½ lb. for 2 shillings). These five years include two when the harvest was bad, and two when it was distinctly good, and can thus be taken as fairly typical of present rates. Averages for earlier years for the Province will be found in table V appended to this article. The ordinary Assamese peasant usually wears home-made articles of dress; the actual cash cost is small, and a woman could probably dress fairly well on Rs. 10 and a man on Rs. 5 per annum. The price of silk clothing is of course considerably higher. A Government orderly spends from Rs. 4 to Rs. 5 a month on his food, including oil, tobacco, spices, salt, and fish. A clerk who shares expenses with one or two friends, need not spend more than Rs. 10 a month on food, including a share of the servants' wages, while the messing charge at the Hindu Hotel at Gauhāti is only Rs. 6 per mensem.

The villagers can, as a rule, obtain nearly all the materials required for their houses free of charge, but if payment must be made a house costs from Rs. 25 to Rs. 50 to construct. The material condition of the people is satisfactory. There is not much serious debt, the great mass of the population is above the necessity of working for daily wages, and the number of people who are in actual want is very small. In upper Assam silk might almost be described as the everyday attire of the women, and there are few houses in which gold ornaments cannot be found. The standard of comfort is not high, but, on the other hand, the villagers are able to satisfy their simple wants with the minimum of toil and trouble. The condition of the clerkly class is not so satisfactory, and those who have no land sometimes have difficulty in suiting their expenditure to their income. The class of landless day labourers is very poorly represented in Assam, and a large number of those who returned themselves under this head at the census were only the younger sons of cultivating families, who take service for short periods in order to earn a little ready money. Their manner of life does not materially differ from that of the poor cultivator, and the two classes merge into one another.

FORESTS.

Area and character.

As might be expected from the character of its surface and climate, the area of forest in Assam is very extensive. Government forests are divided into two classes, the "reserved" and "unclassed state forests," which is the term applied to all waste land at the disposal of the state, although a very large proportion of this is bare of timber. On June 30th 1904, the area of the reserves was 3,778 square miles, and of the unclassed forests 18,509 square miles, excluding most of the Government waste in the Khāsi and Jaintiā, Lushai and Nágá Hills.

The reserved forests of upper and central Assam have not been thoroughly explored, and it is possible that they include tracts in which the tree growth is of an inferior character; but the area of Government waste is so large that the need for disforestation has not yet arisen. In the Surmā Valley the conditions are different. There is a keen demand for land for cultivation, and the people are beginning to press upon the soil. To meet this demand, 28 square miles were recently disforested in Cáchár and 67 square miles in Sylhet, as the land contained little valuable timber. In the hills there is less good forest than might be expected, though there is no lack of wooded country. The habits of the hill races do not permit of the growth of valuable timber except in isolated spots to which their shifting cultivation has not extended; and this cultivation and forest fires have denuded the interior of the hills, where the people chiefly live. The most valuable forests are those of Goálpára, where a large area is covered with *sāl* (*Shorea robusta*). This tree is also found in the Gāro Hills, Kámrūp, Nowgong, and Darrang.

Outside Goálpára and Sylhet, all Districts contain extensive areas of mixed and evergreen forest. Here, besides *sāl*, the most valuable timber trees are *tita sopa* (*Michelia champaca*), *jarul* or *ajhar* (*Lagerstræmia, flos reginæ*), *nahor* (*Mesua ferrea*), *sam* (*Artocarpus chaplasha*), *gomari* (*Gmelina arborea*), *khair* (*Acacia catechu*), *sissu* (*Dalbergia sissoo*), and *gunserai* (*Cinnamomum glanduliferum*). *Nahor* does not grow in the western end of the Assam Valley, though common in the evergreen forests of the Gáro and Khāsi Hills; and *sissu* is not found east of the Manás river.

System of management.

The Goálpára forests were formerly overworked under a wasteful system of levying royalty on the number of axes employed, and when they came under regular management the stock of exploitable timber was found to be nearly exhausted, though there was still a large supply of young trees. A regular working plan has now been introduced. Permits are issued to private persons to fell trees, and a certain quantity of timber is extracted by departmental agency. The forests are situated in the north of the District and some difficulty is experienced in bringing the logs to market, as the rivers are only suitable for transport purposes at certain seasons of the year. This difficulty has, to some extent, been overcome by the purchase of a portable tramway six miles in length. There is also a considerable trade in timber from the permanently settled estates of the District, which lie along both sides of the Brahmaputra, and are thus more favourably situated for purposes of export. The *sāl* forests of the Gáro Hills are valuable, but inaccessible, and it has hitherto been found impossible to work them at a profit on a commercial scale, but there is a considerable trade in canoes hollowed out from large trees which are floated down the Someswari river into Bengal.

Disposal of produce.

In other Districts the only trees of importance as articles of export are *sāl*, *sam*, and *ajhar*, which are floated down the Brahmaputra into Bengal, and from Cáchár into Sylhet, and are chiefly used for boat building. The exploitation of the Cáchár forests for the service of Sylhet has always been active, and is extending, while that of the forests in Goálpára and Kámrūp does not show any marked advance. The upper part of the Assam Valley is remote from any market, and its reserves are hardly touched. Such trade as exists is chiefly in large trees, which are hollowed out and converted into canoes, but of recent years the Assam-Bengal Railway Company have obtained their sleepers from the Nāmbar reserve. *Simul* (*Bombax malabaricum*) and other kinds of soft wood are also largely used in both valleys for the manufacture of tea boxes.

In the Assam Valley trees extracted for sale are felled under a permit specifying their number and name. In Cáchár and Sylhet permits are issued without specifying the quantity or nature of the timber, and royalty is paid at check stations on the river. The trees selected are usually felled early in the year, and the bole is cut into logs from six to seven feet in length, which are carefully dressed with the axe. They are then rolled along to river banks, where they remain till floating is possible, which is usually near the close of the rains, when no danger from flood is anticipated. Where large logs are extracted, elephants are employed to drag them to stacking stations. The heavier kinds of timber, such as *sāl* and *nahor*, are brought down attached to the sides of canoes. All persons holding land direct from Government are permitted to remove from unclassed state forests, without payment, inferior kinds of timber, bamboos, and other forest produce sufficient for their own requirements. The ordinary royalty is levied on forest produce removed for sale. Free grazing is also allowed in unclassed state forests to all cattle that are not kept for dairy or breeding purposes or for sale. The area of Government waste is so extensive that the villagers have no difficulty in satisfying all their wants, and few causes of friction arise. An officer of the Forest department is stationed in nearly every District and acts as the Deputy Commissioner's assistant in forest matters. The management of unclassed state forests in the Assam Valley is in the immediate charge of the subordinate revenue officers, who issue permits for the removal of forest produce. In the Surmā Valley it is entrusted to the subordinate officers of the Forest department. Attempts to protect the forest from fire are restricted to reserved areas and, generally speaking, to forests of *sāl* and other deciduous trees. In 1903-04 special measures were taken with regard to 996·5 square miles, all but 5·3 square miles of which were successfully protected at a cost of Rs. 7,737. 196 square miles were partially protected; no fires occurred in this area during the year.

Minor products. Rubber. The most important minor products are bamboos, canes, reeds, thatching grass, lac and rubber. The rubber tree (*Ficus elastica*) is indigenous in the Darrang, Nowgong and Lakhimpur Districts, but it has been, to a great extent, killed out by excessive and improper tapping. Duty is levied on rubber collected in Government forests, as well as on that brought into Assam from forests beyond the frontier. The total amount realised on account of rubber in 1901 was Rs. 93,000. Artificial plantations of *Ficus elastica* have been started at Kulsi in Kámrūp and at CHARDUAR in the north of Darrang. Opinions still differ as to the comparative advantages of dense and sparse planting, but in the Kulsi plantation, where there are as many as 27 trees to the acre, the average yield per tree exceeded one pound of rubber.

Lac. Lac is not only collected from the forests, but a considerable quantity is cultivated by artificial propagation. The chief seat of the industry is in Kámrūp and the Khási and Jaintiá and Gáro Hills. The lac insect is reared on several species of the *Ficus* family, and the bulk of the produce is exported in the form of stick lac, that is, the small twigs surrounded by deposits of translucent orange yellow gum in which the insect is embedded. Occasionally the gummy matter is scraped from the twigs and separated from the dead bodies of the insects, which are strained off and sold as red dye. The gum is then melted, cleaned, and sold as shell lac or button lac.

The financial working of the Forest department during the past 22 years is shown below :—

		Revenue.	Expenditure.	Surplus.
		Rs.	Rs.	Rs.
Average of 1881-90	...	2,33,487	1,99,488	33,999
„ of 1891-1900	...	4,27,610	2,96,557	1,31,053
1900-1901	...	5,63,400	3,42,963	2,20,437
1903-1904	...	6,76,944	4,51,887	2,25,057

MINES AND MINERALS. Coal. The only minerals in Assam worked on a commercial scale are coal, limestone, and petroleum oil. The most extensive coal measures are those to the south of the Lakhimpur and Sibsāgar Districts, which stretch for a distance of about 110 miles along the north-west face of the Nágá Hills. There are five separate fields, which, running from east to west, are named the Mákum, Jaipur, Názira, Jhānzi, and Disai. The Mákum fields were leased to the Assam Railways and Trading Company in 1881, and a railway was constructed from the Brahmaputra at Dibrugarh to the coal measures on the Dihing. These measures consist of beds of alternating shales, coal, and sandstones. There are altogether five mines worked by the company, who in 1903 employed 1,238 coolies under the supervision of 9 Europeans. No labour is obtainable locally, and the cooly force has to be imported from other parts of India. The ordinary rate of wages is Rs. 7 per mensem for a man and Rs. 6 for a woman. Work is carried on in galleries run into the side of the cliff, the system employed being that known as the square or panel. The bulk of the coal is taken by the India General and Rivers Steam Navigation Companies for use on their steamers, and a small quantity is sold locally to tea gardens. Very little goes to Calcutta. The coal is fairly hard and compact, but after extraction and exposure to the air it breaks up into small pieces. The capital invested in these collieries in 1903 was £ 357,000. The total output in that year was 239,000 tons, as compared with 147,000 tons in 1891. Small quantities of coal have been extracted from the fields to the south of the Sibságar District by the Assam and Singlo Companies for use in their own factories, but not for sale. Coal has also been found in the Gáro and Khási and Jaintiá Hills. The deposits in the Gáro Hills are of cretaceous origin. The principal fields are at Umblay, Rongrengiri, and Darangiri, and for the last-mentioned field a syndicate has taken out a prospecting license. Cretaceous coal has been found in the Khási Hills near Maoflang, about 20 miles south of Shillong, and at Lángrin, on the Jádukáta river. The Maoflang field is worked in a primitive way by the villagers for the supply of the Shillong station. Deposits of tertiary coal have been found in the nummulitic limestone of the southern Khási Hills at Cherrapunji, Lákádong, Thanjinath, Lynkerdem, Maolong, and Mustoh. The Maolong field, which is estimated to contain 15 million tons of coal, has lately been taken on lease by a company. Coal beds have recently been discovered in the vicinity of the Shillong-Gauhāti road about eleven miles north of Shillong; and there are deposits at Langlei and on the Nāmbar river in the Mikīr Hills, but the coal is of poor quality and would hardly pay to work.

Limestone. Next in importance to coal are the vast stores of limestone which exist on the southern face of the Khási and Jaintiá Hills. It is found from the exit of the Someswari river in the Gáro Hills to that of the Hāri river in Jaintiá, but can only be commercially worked where special facilities exist for its transport from the quarries to the kiln. There are altogether 34 tracts which are treated as quarries in the Khási and Jaintiá Hills, one in Sylhet and one in the Gáro Hills. The most important are those situated on the Jādukāta and Panātīrtha rivers, which debouch near Laur in Sylhet, the Dwárā quarries to the east of these, the Shellā quarries on the Bogāpāni, the quarries which lie immediately under Cherrapunji, and the Utma quarries a little to the east on an affluent of the Piyain. The earthquake of 1897 added considerably to the difficulties that had been previously experienced in transporting the stone to a part of the Surmā river navigable by steamers, and in 1903 only eight quarries were worked. The principals are private individuals, the actual quarrymen Khāsis and other local labourers, and no information is available either with regard to the capital invested or the rate of wages paid. The total output in 1903 was 88,675 tons. Limestone is also found in the Mishmi and Mīkīr Hills and in the bed of the Doigrung, a tributary of the Dhansiri, a few miles south of Golāghāt.

Petroleum is only worked on the Mákum fields in Lakhimpur. As early as 1868 a considerable amount of oil was extracted, but no attempt was made to convert the raw product till a small experimental refinery was erected in 1893. In April 1899, the Assam Oil Company was formed with a capital of £ 310,000, and a large refinery was erected at DIGBOI, which in 1903 gave employment to 10 Europeans and 569 natives. In all, 42 wells have been sunk, of which 22 have been abandoned. They vary in depth from 600 to 1,833 feet. The most productive well is said to yield about 50,000 gallons a month. The oil is a crude petroleum, rich in paraffin, and the chief products are light naphthas, kerosene, and wax. The total output in 1903 was 63 tons of candles, 573 tons of paraffin wax, and 1,200,000 gallons of kerosene oil. The oil finds a ready sale locally, but most of the wax goes to England. Petroleum has also been found in the Cáchár District at Māsimpur and Badarpur on the bank of the Barák, and near the Laranga, a little to the north of Kálain. At Khāsimāra, on the southern slopes of the Khási Hills, springs yield oil which recent analysis has shown to be singularly free from wax and of high lubricating power. **Petroleum.**

Iron is still worked, but to a very small extent, in the Khāsi Hills. It is derived from the minute crystals of titaniferous iron ore, which are found in the decomposed granite on the surface of the central dyke of that rock, near the highest portion of the plateau. The iron is of excellent quality, and the industry was formerly one of considerable importance, the metal being exported to the Surmā and Assam Valleys. Large quantities of iron ore used to be extracted from the coal measures in upper Assam under native rule, and iron abounds in the Mīkīr Hills. In the time of the Ahom Rájás, gold was regularly washed from many of the rivers in the Assam Valley, but the industry died out with the disappearance of the native system of compulsory labour. In 1894, a syndicate **Iron, gold, salt, etc.**

was formed and a considerable sum of money expended on the exploration of the rivers of the Lakhimpur District, but gold was not found anywhere in paying quantities, and no return was obtained on the capital embarked in the venture. Salt springs are found in the upper Assam coal area, and in Cáchár and Manipur.

Platinum has been found in the sands of the Dihing river, and lead and silver in the Khamti Hills. Corundum occurs in the Khási Hills, and kaolin in the Gáro and Jaintiá Hills, and near the Brahmakund at the eastern end of the Assam Valley.

ARTS AND MANUFACTURES.

General conditions.

Apart from tea, to which a reference has been already made in the section dealing with agriculture, the Province contains few manufactures of importance. In the Assam Valley and the hills the economic organization of society is of a very simple character. There is no indigenous class of artisans, no specialisation of function, and handicrafts which in other parts of India are confined to special castes, are practised as household industries. The Surmā Valley has passed beyond the stage in which the wants of the household are all supplied by the different members of the family, but artisans are scarce, and manufactured products are, as a rule, imported from beyond the frontier. Such as they are, the industries of most importance are the burning of limestone, the weaving of cotton and silk cloth, the preparation of molasses and mustard oil, the making of boats, canoes, and tea boxes, the refining of crude petroleum, and the manufactures of metal and earthen vessels, rough iron implements, and native jewellery.

Cotton cloth.

The weaving of cotton cloth is still largely practised by the natives of Assam proper. The work is entirely carried on by women, and in almost every house is to be found a loom, on which most of the clothes worn by the members of the family are prepared, but these articles are chiefly intended for home use, and only an insignificant quantity is produced for sale. Weaving forms one of the most essential part of a girl's education, and skill in this art does much to enhance the value of a bride. Among the well-to-do, home-made cotton cloths are being displaced by imported goods, and the ladies of the family confine themselves to the production of fine cloths, embroidered and enriched with borders of silk or gold and silver thread. In the Surmā Valley weaving was never a home industry, and was confined to the professional weaving castes, but most of these have now abandoned their traditional occupation for agriculture, and the great mass of the population are clothed in imported fabrics. The hillman's clothing, on the other hand, is usually home made, and the cloths, though rough, are generally dyed a rich blue or red, the necessary ingredients being readily obtained from the surrounding jungle.*

Silk.

A more characteristic industry of the Assam Valley is the rearing of silkworms and the manufacture of cloth from their

* For further details see "Monograph on the Cotton Fabrics of Assam," Calcutta, 1897.

thread. There are four varieties of domesticated worm in use. The smaller or multivoltine *pāt* worm (*Bombyx cræsi*) and the larger or univoltine worm of the same name (*Bombyx textor*) are both fed on the mulberry, and produce a fine white thread. The *mūgā* worm (*Antheræa Assamæa*) is usually reared on the *sum* tree (*Machilus odoratissima*), and yields a yellowish buff silk with a rich gloss, but if fed on the *chapa* (*Magnolia Griffithii*) and the *mezankuri* (*Tetranthera polyantha*), it spins a very fine white cocoon. The *eri* worm (*Attacus ricini*) is so called from its attachment to the castor-oil plant (*Ricinus communis*) though it also feeds on various other trees. The matrix of *eri* silk is extremely gummy, and the thread has to be spun from the cocoon. The white cloth made of *pāt* silk is an article of luxury, and is not easily procured, but *mūgā* silk is largely used by the women of all classes of society in upper and central Assam, and as a holiday dress by men. It is also exported to the hill Districts, where it is much appreciated by the Khásis, Garos, and other tribes. *Eri* cloth is of a drab colour, and, though often coarse in texture, is very durable. It is light, but warm, and the ordinary cold-weather wrap of the Assamese villager is generally made of this silk. The manufacture of both *mūgā* and *eri* cloth is purely domestic. There are no large filatures, nor is there any system of breeding the worms on an extensive scale, and all attempts made so far to practise sericulture on a commercial scale have ended in failure. The villager rears silkworms enough to yield him a few ounces of thread, which he either gets his women folk to weave or sells at the village fair. In upper Assam there is not much trade in silk, but in the western Districts the animistic tribes often obtain the cash required for their land revenue by selling *eri* cloths to the Bhotiās and other tribes inhabiting the lower ranges of the Himālayas, or to Mārwāri merchants for export to Calcutta. Proposals have recently been made for the development of the silk industry among the Khásis and in Manipur, and are now under consideration.

Jewellery.

The jewellery made in the Province does not, as a rule, possess much merit, but really artistic necklaces of gold filigree work are produced at Barpetá, and the enamelled lockets and ear ornaments of Jorhāt are not unpleasing. The enamel, which is usually a rich green or blue, is laid on between thin gold wire on a basis of lac, and is set with cheap garnets and false rubies. The Khásis wear bracelets, necklaces and coronets of silver and gold. They are handsome articles, but somewhat heavy in design. The industry is not of any great importance, and is only followed by a few persons, most of whom have some other means of livelihood.

Metal work and pottery.

Other manufactures include brass and bell-metal utensils, iron work, and rough pottery. The articles produced possess no artistic merit, and the local supply has to be supplemented by importation from Bengal. Bell-metal utensils are cast in moulds. Brass vessels are hammered out of thin sheets of that metal. The industry in the Assam Valley is largely in the hands of the Moriás, a class of degraded Muhammadans, who are said to be the descendants of prisoners captured by the Ahoms when Turbak was defeated in 1532A.D. Under native rule the smelting of iron ore was a considerable industry. The chronicles of the Muhammadan invasions frequently refer to the large numbers of cannon possessed by the enemy, and these guns, some of them of great weight and size, are found scattered over the Assam Valley at the present day. Buchanan Hamilton, writing at the beginning of the last century, makes mention of a valuable iron mine south of Jorhát, and the remains of iron workings are to be seen all over the Khási Hills. Iron working, however, like other industries, has died out since the pressure of necessity has been removed, though the Khásis still smelt small quantities of ore, which they convert into bill hooks and other implements of agriculture. Other blacksmiths are usually foreigners, who work with imported metal, which they forge into bill hooks, sickles, and ploughshares, but the industry has few followers and is of little importance. Pottery, which is of the simplest kind, is either made by Kumhárs on the wheel, or by Hiras, who beat out the clay to a thin sheet, and lay one strip upon another till the vessel is complete.

Sylhet specialities. The most important manufacture of Sylhet, after tea, is lime, which is burnt on the banks of the Surmā river. Other specialities of the District are mats made of bamboo and reeds, boxes and furniture made of reeds, leaf umbrellas, bracelets of shell and lac, *agar* or *attar*, a perfume distilled from the resinous sap of the *agar* tree, children's toys, fish oil, dried fish and boats. Iron work inlaid with brass, lac inlaid with feathers and talc, and ivory fans and chessmen used formerly to be manufactured, but these arts are now in a very languishing condition.

Other manufactures. Of recent years there has been some extension of the mustard oil and sugar industries in the Province. At Gauháti two mills, worked by steam, are capable of turning out over 3 tons of oil a day; but oilmen are generally foreigners, who use the ordinary bullock mill of upper India. Sugarcane is still, as a rule, crushed between two wooden rollers, in spite of the superior advantages of the Bihiā mill, and the juice is converted into raw molasses. Boat building is carried on in Sylhet, and more than a hundred years ago the Collector of that District built a ship of 400 tons burthen, drawing 17 feet when fully loaded. In the Assam Valley canoes are manufactured out of trees, which are hollowed out till only an outer skin about one inch and a quarter in thickness remains. If a large boat is required, the shell is plastered over with mud and steamed over a fire, and the sides are then distended by the insertion of thwarts.

The arts of carving in ivory and wood are almost extinct. Wood carvers are generally carpenters by profession, and even their best work is usually very rough: carved ivory can only be obtained, on order, at Jorhât, Barpetá, and Sylhet.

Apart from tea and the petroleum refinery, to which reference has been already made, the only industries in which European capital is embarked are saw-mills and the brick and pottery works at Ledo in the Lakhimpur District. There were altogether 11 saw-mills in 1903, which gave employment to 1,205 persons. The bulk of the output consists of tea boxes, which are generally made from the wood of the *simul* tree (*Bombax malabaricum*). In spite of the large local demand for this commodity, the industry is in a somewhat stagnant condition, as foreign-made boxes are much in favour with the agents in Calcutta. In 1903 149 persons were employed in the pottery works.

COMMERCE AND TRADE

Trade with the Province prior to annexation

The first mention of the trade of Sylhet is to be found in the memoirs of Mr. Lindsay, who was appointed Collector of that District in 1778A.D. The principal exports at that time were lime, elephants, iron, silk, coarse muslins, ivory, honey, gums, drugs and oranges. For the Assam Valley records are fuller, thanks to the Muhammadan invaders. In the 17th century the Ahom rulers seem to have adopted a policy of isolation and forbade people either to enter or leave their territories, and trade was carried on by a caravan, which proceeded once a year to Gauháti with gold, musk, *agar*, pepper and silk, and exchanged these products for salt, saltpetre, sulphur, and other articles. At the end of the 18th century, the trade of the valley was in the hands of two men, who farmed the customs and established a monopoly at Hadira, on the north bank of the Brahmaputra, nearly opposite Goálpára. On the British side there was a colony of European merchants, who had forcibly seized the monopoly of the trade from Bengal; and unsatisfactory though these arrangements were, the volume of business declined, on our occupation of the Province, owing to the abolition of the monopoly and the bad faith of the individual Assamese merchants. The imports, which consisted almost entirely of salt, were valued at 2¼ lakhs of rupees; the exports at 4¾ lakhs, three-fourths of which represented the price of lac, and the greater part of the remainder that of silk, mustard-seed, and cotton.

General character of trade.

At the present day, the trade of Assam is carried on in two different directions; first and chiefly with the neighbouring Province of Bengal; and secondly with the tribes on the northern and eastern frontier. The economic organization of the Province is still in a very undeveloped state, and apart from tea, the bulk of the exports consists of raw products. The imports include manufactured goods, but as Assam does not produce enough grain to feed its large foreign population, there is also a large admixture of food stuffs. The principal imports are cotton piece-goods and twist, husked rice, salt, sugar, kerosene, mustard and other oils, gram and pulse, tobacco, and metals. The chief exports are tea, unhusked rice, oil-seeds, coal and lime, timber, jute, raw cotton, lac, hides, oranges and caoutchouc. The backward condition of the Province is illustrated by the fact that it exports unhusked rice and oil-seeds and imports mustard oil and husked rice. Nearly all the rice exported goes from the Surmā Valley, which in normal years produces more than is required for local consumption. The imported rice goes to upper Assam, where the proportion of garden coolies is very large.

Centres of trade. The most important permanent centres of trade are GOALPARA, BARPETA, GAUHATI, TEZPUR, NOWGONG, GOLAGHAT, JORHAT, DIBRUGARH, and SADIYA in the Assam Valley, and HABIGANJ, AJMIRIGANJ, SUNAMGANJ, CHHATAK, BALAGANJ, SYLHET and SILCHAR in the valley of the Surmā.

Mechanism of internal trade. None of these places is, however, of great importance, as the tea industry has a very decentralizing effect upon the internal commerce of Assam. All over the Province weekly markets are held on stated days, where buyers and sellers meet, and most of the business is done. The classes who conduct the trade differ in the two valleys. In both, tea, the great export of Assam, is consigned straight from the gardens where it is produced to Calcutta, either to be sold there or shipped to England for sale, though a small but increasing proportion of the crop is now exported from Chittagong, where it is conveyed by the Assam-Bengal Railway. A considerable share of the export trade in mustard from the Assam Valley is in the hands of a class of traders who are natives of the Kámrūp District, but almost all the rest of the export traffic, and nearly the whole of the import traffic of the valley, is carried on by Mārwāri traders, who are usually known as "Kayahs." There are in addition a few Bengali Muhammadans in the larger towns, who sell furniture, haberdashery, and oilman's stores; but the Kayahs monopolize the banking and wholesale business of the valley, and their shops are to be found not only in the chief business centres, but on every tea garden and on the paths by which the hillmen bring down their cotton, rubber, lac, and other products. The Assamese have no commercial aptitude, and have thus allowed the whole of the profits of the trade of their country to pass into the hands of foreigners. In the Surmā Valley the conditions are somewhat different. The native population contains a large trading element, and merchants from Dacca are more numerous than in Assam proper. A fair number of Mārwāris are found, but in no sense do they dominate the trade of the valley.

The hill men. Except among the Khásis and a few of the Nágá tribes, the number of hillmen who are entirely dependent upon trade for their support is small. Most tribes, however, grow articles like cotton, chillies, and lac for export, and bring them to the markets at the foot of the hills, where they exchange them for rice, salt, dried fish, cloth and petty oilman's stores. This trade is largely carried on by barter. The tricks of the petty shopkeeper are not unknown; the cotton is often watered to increase its weight, and stones embedded in the rubber. The Khásis and Angāmī Nágás are keen and energetic traders, and sometimes go as far afield as Calcutta in search of goods. Manipur exports rice, timber, and bamboos and till recently exported tea-seed and cattle. Timber and other forest produce is floated down the rivers into Cāchār, but grain and other goods go by cart road to Dimāpur, a station on the Assam-Bengal Railway.

Trade with other parts of India.

Almost the whole of the trade of Assam with other parts of India is carried on with Bengal, principally with Calcutta, that with other Provinces being less than one per cent. of the whole. The principal exports and imports have already been mentioned above, and statistics showing their value will be found in table VI appended to this article. The great bulk of the goods are still carried by river, though in the Surmā Valley the amount carried by the Assam-Bengal Railway is increasing year by year. River-borne trade from the Assam Valley goes chiefly by steamer; but in the Surmā Valley, and especially in Sylhet, country boats are largely employed. There is very little road traffic between Assam and Bengal, and the only commodities brought into the Province by road are cattle, ponies, sheep, and other live stock.

Trade outside India.

Foreign trade is carried on with Bhután, Towang, and the tribes inhabiting the lower Himālayan hills and the eastern end of the Assam Range. The Bhotiás of Bhután and Towang bring down their goods on sturdy little ponies to fairs held at Darrangā and SUBANKHATA in the north of Kámrūp, and at UDALGURI and Ghágrápára in Darrang, and spread from these centres over the surrounding country. The trade is largely carried on by barter, and the statistics which are collected by the local police and revenue officials must be received with caution. The tribes to the east export little but rubber, which is carried down by coolies, the chief markets being Tezpur, North Lakhimpur and Sadiyā. Elsewhere the principal imports are rubber, wax, and ponies, the exports cotton cloth and yarn and silk. The total foreign trade is, however, only worth about 4 lakhs of rupees per annum.

MEANS OF COMMUNICATION.

The Assam-Bengal Railway.

The principal railway of Assam is the Assam-Bengal Railway, which runs from the port of Chittagong to Silchar at the eastern end of the Surmā Valley. A second branch of the same line runs along the south of the Assam Valley from Gauhāti to Tinsukiā, a station on the Dibru-Sadiyā railway, and is connected with the Surmā Valley branch by a line that pierces the North Cāchār hills, the points of junction being Lumding in the northern and Badarpur in the southern valley. Work was begun on this railway in 1891, and five years later a length of about 115 miles from

Chándurá to Badarpur was opened to traffic; but the hill section has presented difficulties of a most exceptional character, and was not finally completed till the end of 1903. This section runs for the most part through shale of the worst description, often intermixed with bands of kaolinite, which swells when exposed and causes heavy slips, or exerts immense pressure on the sides of tunnels. To counteract this pressure, very heavy masonry was required, cuttings had to be arched in, and special measures taken to allow the drainage to escape. Though the hill section is only 113 miles in length, it contains 24 tunnels, 7 covered ways, and 74 major bridges, the longest being 650 feet, and the highest 113 feet above the river bed; while many of the banks and cuttings approach 100 feet in height and depth respectively. Apart from the special engineering difficulties, great inconvenience was experienced, owing to the absence of local labour and food supplies, and to the unhealthiness of the country traversed. At one time, in addition to the railway material, food for more than 25,000 men had to be carried into the hills on elephants, bullocks, ponies, and other pack animals. The result is that the cost of construction of the hill section has been extremely heavy. The principal engineering difficulties in the plains were the bridge, 500 yards in length, which crosses the Kapili and the marshes which fringe its banks; and the bridge over the Barák at Badarpur, which, though shorter, was even more costly, as its foundations were carried 80 feet below the river bed. The line, which is on the metre gauge, has a total length within the Province of 571 miles, and has been constructed by a company working under a Government guarantee. The bulk of the capital has, however, been found by Government.

Minor railways. A small line of great commercial importance is that running from the steamer port at DIBRUGARH to MARGHERITA, with a branch to Táláp. The total length is only 78 miles, but it taps a large number of flourishing tea gardens, and affords an outlet for the coal and oil of Mákum to the Brahmaputra. It was constructed on the metre-gauge system by a private company, assisted with a Government guarantee, and was opened in 1885. The same year saw the completion of a small state railway in the Sibságar District, running from Kakilámukh on the Brahmaputra to Mariáni and Titābar, which was originally built for the convenience of the numerous tea gardens in the neighbourhood, as the unmetalled road to the river became almost impassable to wheeled traffic in the rains. The total length is 30 miles, and the gauge 2 feet. Similar considerations led to the construction of a light railway on the 2′ 6″ gauge, from TEZPUR ghāt in the Darrang District to BALIPARA, a distance of 20 miles. The line was built in 1895 by a private company, but receives a small subsidy from the local board. The only other open line in the Province is the branch of the Eastern

Bengal State Railway, which connects Dhubri with the Bengal system, and was opened for traffic in 1902. Fifteen miles of this line, which is on the metre gauge, lie within the boundaries of Assam.

Sufficient time has not yet elapsed for the effects produced by the completion of the Assam-Bengal Railway to be fully seen. Silchar, which was formerly extremely inaccessible in the dry season, has been brought within 33 hours of Calcutta; and it is hoped that population may pass by the hill section from the densely peopled plains of Sylhet to the extensive tracts of good land now lying waste in the Assam Valley. A line from Golakganj near Dhubri to Gauháti is under construction, and there will soon be through railway communication between the eastern end of the Brahmaputra Valley and the more densely populated parts of India from which the Province draws its labour. **Effect of railways.**

In 1891, only 114 miles of railway were open in the Province; by 1903 the figure had risen to 715 miles, 617 miles of which represented the mileage of state lines. The total capital which by 1903 had been expended on the minor railways, the whole of which lie within the boundaries of the Province, *i.e.*, the Dibru-Sadiyā, Tezpur-Bālipára, and Jorhát railways, was Rs. 94,69,000. In that year 567,000 passengers and 317,000 tons of goods and minerals were carried by these railways: the gross working expenses were Rs. 5,95,000, and the net revenue yielded 5 per cent. on the capital employed.

The excellence of its water communications makes Assam less dependent upon its highways than other parts of India, and it was not till 1865 that steps were taken to construct a road through the whole length of the Brahmaputra Valley. This road runs along the south bank of the river from Sadiyā at the eastern end to a point opposite Dhubri, where it is connected by a steam ferry with the road system of Goálpára and northern Bengal. At Gauháti it is joined by an excellent metalled road which runs to Shillong. Shillong is connected *viâ* Cherrapunji, Therriāghāt, Companyganj, and Sylhet with Cáchár, though for a distance of about 8 miles down the face of the Khási Hills, which here rise very sharply from the plains, the tract is not fit for wheeled traffic. From Cáchár a bridle path leads to Manipur, and from there a cart road to the Brahmaputra, passing through Kohīmā, Dimápur (a station on the Assam-Bengal Railway), and Golághát. A second trunk road runs along the north bank of the Brahmaputra, but through the greater part of its length does not carry much traffic. The main arteries of trade are, however, the rivers, and since recently the Assam-Bengal Railway, and the most important roads are those leading to the steamer ghāts or railway stations. Numerous roads have also been made in the tea Districts **Roads.**

connecting the various plantations with one another and with the main lines of communication, whether water, road, or railway. Apart from the trunk roads, the most important routes are:—the road from Turá in the Gáro Hills to the Brahmaputra, the road that runs from north Gauháti to Darrangā, at the foot of the Bhután hills, the roads from Rangámátighāt to the north of Mangaldai subdivision, the road from Sibságar to Disāngmukh on the Brahmaputra, and the Dhodar Alī, which runs along the south of the Sibságar District. In the Surmá Valley two important roads are those from Sylhet to Fenchuganj, and thence to Kulaurā railway station, and from Silchar up the Hailákándi valley.

Road mileage. Generally speaking, there has not been much change during the past ten years, but the route to Manipur was first made passable for carts after the outbreak of 1891. The ordinary bullock carts of upper India are in common use in the Assam Valley, but here and there carts are still to be found whose wheels consist of solid discs of wood. In the Surmá Valley carts are very scarce, and heavy goods are chiefly carried by boat and to some extent by pack bullock. A primitive form of wheel-less sledge is sometimes used for the transport of agricultural produce. In 1890-91 there were 293 miles of Imperial, 2,119 miles of Provincial, and 3,095 miles of local fund roads, and the cost of maintenance was Rs. 4,70,000. In 1903-04 the figure for Provincial roads was 1,625 miles and for local fund roads 4,483 miles, and the cost of maintenance was Rs. 8,87,000. Inspection bungalows are provided at intervals of ten or twelve miles along all the main roads, but they contain nothing but a few tables and chairs and bedsteads, and the occupant must provide servants, food, and cooking utensils. The cost of metalling in Assam is very heavy. This is partly due to the high rate of wages prevailing, partly to the difficulty experienced in obtaining material. In 1903-04 there were only 144 miles of metalled road, most of which lay in the hills. Avenues are not planted on the roads.

Water communication. The chief means of communication in Assam are still its waterways. The Brahmaputra is navigable by large steamers to within a few miles of Dibrugarh, and carries most of the trade of the Assam Valley. In the rains tea and other produce are brought down the tributaries that flow into it on either side, though the river ports are always connected by roads with the interior. The Surmá Valley is a network of streams, and in the rainy season the western part of the Sylhet District lies almost entirely under water. A large fleet of steamers maintained by the India General Steam Navigation Company and the Rivers Steam Navigation Company plies on the rivers of both valleys. A daily service of passenger boats runs from Goalundo to Dibrugarh. Since the construction of the Assam-Bengal Railway the timing has been accelerated, and the journey up is now performed in four and a half and that down in three and a quarter days, but in the cold weather fogs are sometimes a serious obstacle to traffic. A considerable amount of cargo is carried in these vessels, but special cargo steamers with large flats also run, and carry goods, the bulk of which renders them unsuitable for carriage by the smaller and more speedy passenger boats. In the Surmā Valley large steamers run to Silchar in the rainy season, but in the cold weather cannot proceed beyond Fenchuganj. Small feeder steamers ply on the minor rivers in both valleys. Ordinary native boats, which, when the wind is not favourable, are generally towed up-stream, are largely used in the Surmá Valley and to some extent in lower Assam. The typical Assamese craft consists, however, of a canoe hollowed out of a large trunk of wood. Steam ferries are maintained on the Brahmaputra at Dhubri and Gauháti. Elsewhere, the river is crossed in canoes, or rafts made by fastening two or three canoes side by side and laying planks across them, and in the rains the passage sometimes occupies more than twelve hours. Most of the minor streams on the important roads are bridged, but a large number of ferries have still to be kept open.

For postal purposes the Province has been formed into a circle under a Deputy Postmaster-General. The following statistics show the advance in postal business since the year 1880-81:— **Post office.**

—	1880-81.	1890-91.	1900-01.	1903-04.
Number of post offices	145	276	314	344
Number of letter-boxes	107	195	423	452
Number of miles of postal communication.	2,221	3,815	4,230	4,576¼
Total number of postal articles delivered—				
Letters	2,115,130	2,001,462	4,979,070	5,044,936
Postcards	249,895	1,284,826	3,006,531	3,437,122
Packets	59,018	338,876	965,711 (Including unregistered newspapers).	872,586
Newspapers	417,742	755,785	1,049,453 (Registered as newspapers in the Post Office).	943,251
Parcels	37,256	74,903	136,406	173,904
Value of stamps sold to the public ...	Rs. 82,869	Rs. 2,04,475	Rs. 2,44,198	Rs. 2,58,583
Value of money orders issued ...	„ 13,46,130	„ 52,11,700	„ 98,76,590	„ 92,98,498
Total amount of Savings Bank deposits	...	„ 13,99,347	„ 30,74,356	„ 36,28,721

The figures given above relate to both the Imperial post and the local or District post. The latter system is maintained by local boards to provide postal communication between the headquarters of Districts and subdivisions, and revenue and police stations in the interior, in cases where the maintenance of the necessary lines of communication would not be warranted by the commercial principles of the post office. The expenditure from local funds averaged Rs. 48,000 per annum for the five years ending with 1902-03. The number of District post offices on the 31st March 1904 was 58, and the total mileage of District post mail lines 1,387.

GOVERNMENT AND ADMINISTRATIVE DIVISIONS.*

General administrative staff.

The administration of the Province is entrusted to a Chief Commissioner acting immediately under the orders of the Government of India. His general executive staff consists of (1) the Assam Commission, which has a sanctioned strength of 41, and is composed of members of the Covenanted Civil Service, with a certain proportion of officers deputed from the Indian Army; (2) the Provincial Service, which has a sanctioned strength of 36, and is a body of subordinate magistrates recruited in India, most of whom are natives of that country; and (3) the Subordinate Civil Service, which has a sanctioned strength of 52, and consists of native officers, most of whom are employed in the land revenue department.

As in other parts of India, the unit of administration is the District, the area in charge of a District Magistrate, or Deputy Commissioner as he is called, who is responsible for the collection of the revenue, the administration of justice, the preservation of order, and the harmonious working of all the departments of Government within its boundaries. There are altogether 12 Districts in the Province, with an average area of 4,435 square miles and an average population of 486,823. The six Districts in the Assam Valley have been formed into a Division under the general control of a Commissioner, but elsewhere the Chief Commissioner performs the functions of Commissioner of Division. The District is again divided into subdivisions, of which there are 27, including two Districts which have none, the average area of each subdivision being 1,971 square miles, and the average population 216,366. The District Magistrate, who is allowed one or more assistants, holds direct charge of the headquarters subdivision, and each outlying subdivision is entrusted to a magistrate, who is usually a European, subordinate to the Deputy Commissioner. This magistrate is, however, invested with a considerable measure of responsibility, as within his jurisdiction he exercises, subject to the control of the Deputy Commissioner, most of the functions of that officer. The smallest unit of administration in the Assam Valley was originally the mauza, an area for which an officer called the mauzadār

* For the changes made in 1905 in this and the following section, see EASTERN BENGAL AND ASSAM

contracted to pay the revenue. Between 1883 and 1896 the majority of these mauzas were formed into tahsīls, which were placed in charge of salaried officers of higher rank, and which have an average area of 211 square miles and an average population of 47,000 souls. Economy was the principal motive of this change, but experience showed that the reduction in expenditure was not as great as had originally been anticipated. The mauzadāri system is more popular with the villagers, and has the additional advantage of creating a body of men who, while accepted by the people as their leaders, are bound to Government by the facts of their position. It has accordingly been decided gradually to abolish the existing tahsīls, and again entrust the duty of collection to the mauzadār. In the temporarily settled tracts it is the tahsīldār or the mauzadār who represents the Government in its most direct and visible form to the mass of the people. Elsewhere in the plains the police are brought most closely into contact with the villagers in rural areas.

Village autonomy. In the two valleys the houses of the cultivators are scattered over a wide area, and the village organization was never very strong. Some authority was, however, exercised by the rural council, or *mel* or *panchāyat*, and, though not recognised by our courts, its decisions are often accepted as binding by the parties concerned. In the hills the authority of the village headmen is greater; they are held responsible for the preservation of law and order, and are empowered to dispose of petty criminal and civil cases. The persons entrusted with the duty of collecting the house-tax, which takes the place of land revenue in the hills, are called laskars in the Gáro Hills, dollois and sardārs in the Khási and Jaintiá Hills, and lambardārs among the Nágás.

The various departments. The Chief Commissioner is further assisted in the administration of the Province by selected officers, who are responsible to him for the various departments committed to their charge. The appointments of Inspector General of Police, Prisons and Registration, and Superintendent of Stamps are held by a member of the Assam Commission of the standing of a Deputy Commissioner. Till recently he was also Commissioner of Excise, but the charge of this department has now been transferred to the Commissioner in the Assam Valley, and to the Chief Commissioner in the Surmá Valley and hill Districts. Another officer of the standing of a Deputy Commissioner is in charge of the department of Land Records and Agriculture. Public Works are entrusted to a Superintending Engineer, who also acts as Secretary to the Chief Commissioner in that department, and has under him a staff of Executive and Assistant Engineers and native subordinates. The Education department is managed by a Director of Public Instruction, who is assisted by 2

Inspectors, 19 Deputy and 15 Sub-Inspectors of Schools. The Medical department consists of a Sanitary Commissioner, who is also the Principal Medical Officer of the Assam garrison, 9 Civil Surgeons belonging to the Indian Medical Service, and a certain number of Military or Civil Assistant Surgeons. The Forest department is under the control of a Conservator assisted by a suitable staff. The Civil accounts of the Province are in charge of a Comptroller, who is directly subordinate to the Financial Department of the Government of India. The Post Office is administered by a Deputy Postmaster-General, and the Telegraph department by a Superintendent. These two officers are not, however, under the orders of the Chief Commissioner.

Native States. The only Native State of any importance under the control of the Assam Administration is MANIPUR. After the outbreak of 1891, a young boy, who was a member of a collateral line, was placed upon the throne, and during his minority the administration has been conducted by a member of the Assam Commission, who acts as Political Agent and Superintendent of the State. Advantage has been taken of this opportunity to introduce various reforms, and the system of administration has been in some ways assimilated to that prevailing in British territory. The native courts have, however, been retained, and the arrangements for the assessment and collection of land revenue are of necessity of a somewhat simple character. The States in the Khási Hills are of no importance, and the system of administration does not differ materially from that in force in other hill Districts.

LEGISLATION AND JUSTICE.

System of Legislation. The ordinary method by which measures of legislation are brought into force in the Province is that common to other parts of India, by which Acts are passed after full debate in the Council of the Governor General for making Laws and Regulations, which apply to Assam as well as to other parts of the Indian Empire. Provision has also been made for the enactment of Regulations suited to the peculiar necessities of the Province, and the Chief Commissioner is empowered to propose to the Governor General in Council drafts of any such Regulations as seem to him to be required. These Regulations, after they have been approved by the executive Council of the Governor General, and after they have received his assent, are published in the *Gazette of India*, and thereupon have the force of law. The Chief Commissioner has also power, with the previous assent of the Governor General in Council, to extend to the Province any measures passed by other local Legislatures which appear to him to be suited to its requirements.

The most important Acts of the Governor General in Council which have come into force in Assam since 1880 are the

Vaccination Act, XIII of 1880; the Labour Immigration Act, I of 1882, which was superseded by Act VI of 1901; and the Civil Courts Act, XII of 1887. The Regulations proposed by the Chief Commissioner which have received the assent of the Governor General in Council are the Frontier Tracts Regulation, II of 1880, the Assam Land and Revenue Regulation, I of 1886, the Assam Military Police Regulation, IV of 1890, the Sylhet *Jhum* Regulation, III of 1891, and the Assam Forest Regulation, VII of 1891. The following important Acts of the Bengal Council have also been extended to Assam:—The Public Demands Recovery Act, VII of 1880, the Municipal Act, III of 1884, and the Private Fisheries Act, II of 1889.

Stipendiary Magistrates are the foundation of the system of criminal administration in the plains, for, though a few Honorary Magistrates have been appointed, the total amount of work done by them is inconsiderable. Appeals from their decisions lie to the Judge, except in the case of Magistrates with second and third class powers, from whom there is an appeal to the Deputy Commissioner. In both valleys there is a Sessions Judge, from whom appeals lie to the High Court of Fort William in Bengal. Petty civil cases in the Assam Valley are heard by Assistant or Extra Assistant Commissioners, who exercise the powers of Munsiffs. Above them come the District Magistrates, who act as Subordinate Judges, while the Sessions Judge is also the Civil Judge of the valley. In Cāchār, the same system is in force, the powers of the District Judge of Cāchār being vested in the District Judge of Sylhet. In the latter District, civil work is in charge of the District and Sessions Judge assisted by two Subordinate Judges and a staff of Munsiffs. In the hill Districts and certain frontier tracts the High Court has no jurisdiction except in criminal matters over European British subjects, and the Chief Commissioner is himself the highest appellate authority in criminal and civil cases. The Deputy Commissioner exercises the combined powers of District and Sessions Judge and Magistrate of a District, and the Assistant Commissioners and Extra Assistant Commissioners the powers of Magistrates and Munsiffs. Judicial powers are also exercised by the local chiefs in the Khāsi and Lushai Hills. Criminal and Civil Justice.

Table VII annexed to this article shows the amount of work done by the criminal and civil courts of the Province during recent years. The increase in criminal work is principally due to an increase in the number of cases under special Acts, such as the Labour Acts, XIII of 1859 and I of 1882, the Cattle Trespass Act, the Excise Act, the Municipal Act, and the Police Act. Appeals were preferred in 1903 by rather more than 36 per cent. of the persons on whom appealable sentences were passed in the criminal courts, and of these, 74 per cent. of the appeals to the

Sessions Court and 59 per cent. of those to District Magistrate were entirely unsuccessful.

There has been little increase in civil business except under the head of title and other suits, and rent suits in Sylhet. The great majority of suits are for small sums, and in 1903 the value of about 84 per cent of the total number instituted did not exceed Rs. 100. It is seldom, moreover, that the claim is disputed, and 79 per cent. of the cases were either withdrawn or compromised, or decided *ex-parte*. Appeals were preferred in 1903 against 33 per cent. of the appealable decrees passed by Subordinate Judges and 28 per cent. of those passed by Munsiffs, but in only 15 per cent. of the cases heard was the order of the lower court reversed. The readiness of the people to assert their rights can be judged from the fact that 21 per cent. of the appeals to the High Court at Calcutta were valued at less than Rs. 50.

Registration. The Inspector General of Police and Prisons is also Inspector General of Registration, and he holds besides the offices of Registrar of Joint Stock Companies under the Companies Act, and of Registrar General of Births, Deaths, and Marriages under Act VI of 1886. All Deputy Commissioners are Registrars in their respective Districts. In the Brahmaputra Valley the Sub-Registrars are Magistrates subordinate to the Deputy Commissioner, who do this work in addition to their own duties. In the Surmá Valley there are special Sub-Registrars at the headquarters of all subdivisions and rural Sub-Registrars at various centres. The Registration Act is not in force in the hills. The number of documents registered in 1881-90 (average) was 19,700, in 1891-1900 (average) 36,500 and in 1903, 55,400. The number of offices open in that year was 29. Between 1881 and 1890 the average number open was 21.

FINANCE.

Taxation prior to British Rule. Little is known about the system of taxation in force in Sylhet under native rule. It is said that in 1582 A.D. the revenue was assessed at nearly 1¾ lakhs of rupees;* but Mr. Lindsay, who was Collector there in 1778 A.D., reported that under Mughal rule the District yielded little revenue beyond a few elephants, spices, and wood, and most of the local receipts seem to have been devoted to the up-keep of a military establishment to protect the frontier.† In 1776, Mr. Holland settled the District for 2½ lakhs of rupees, which were paid in cowries at the rate of 5,120 to the rupee, but great difficulty was experienced in realizing this assessment. The rates of land revenue assessed in Cāchār before it lapsed to the East India Company varied from 10 annas to R. 1-4-0 per acre. and in addition to this the cultivators were expected to provide the labour required for the Rājā's works, while trade was hampered by customs, monopolies, and market dues. The Ahom government was

* Principal Heads of the History and Statistics of the Dacca Division, p. 292, Calcutta, 1866.

† Lives of the Lindsays, London, 1849, p. 163.

based upon a system of organized forced labour. Each male free man above 16 years of age was styled a *paik*. The *paiks* were grouped in bodies of three or four, termed *gots*, one of whom was always supposed to be engaged on public duty, and was supported while so employed by the remaining members of his *got*. Over each hundred *gots* there was an officer called *saikya*, and over every ten *saikyas* a *hazāri*. The whole population was thus organized either for military or industrial enterprise, and this fine supply of disciplined labour enabled the Rājās to construct the great public works which remain to be the wonder of an age when coolies can only be procured with great expense and difficulty. Groups of *paiks* were also assigned to the various industries then practised in the Province. The wants of the royal household were supplied by guilds of farmers, silk weavers, gold washers, oil pressers, fishermen, and other artizans. The ministers and the Brāhmans received allotments of land and of peasants to cultivate it, and all adult males were liable to compulsory military service. The people supplied the government and the chief families with everything they required free of cost, and there was thus little necessity for a money tax, though sums were collected in the shape of poll-tax and revenue for land occupied by the peasants in excess of the free grant given to them in return for their service to the state.

Provincial contracts. The system of Provincial contracts was first introduced in 1871, when Assam formed part of Bengal, and in 1878 the contract with Assam was revised, as it was found necessary to provide funds to meet growing expenditure. The Province received the whole of the revenue from excise, Provincial rates, stamps, registration, law and justice, police, education, and a few minor heads, together with 20 per cent. of the land revenue; while it undertook entire responsibility for the charges pertaining to these departments, and for charges connected with administration and Provincial public works.

The contract of 1882. In the settlement of 1882 the system of the receipts and charges under excise, stamps, and registration, which were formerly entirely Provincial, were equally divided between Provincial and Imperial, and similar treatment was accorded to the Forest budget. Sixty-three per cent. of the land revenue receipts was allotted to Provincial, together with a corresponding liability for the charges. The Provincial receipts were estimated to amount to Rs. 44,77,000 per annum, and the normal expenditure to Rs. 43,68,000. A margin was thus left for the growing needs of the Administration. During the currency of this contract there was a satisfactory expansion of the revenue, and the additional funds which were thus rendered available enabled the Administration to increase the efficiency of nearly every department of Government. Considerable expenditure was incurred on surveys, and on the improvement of the frontier police force. New dispensaries were opened, the construction of the Jorhāt and Cherra-Companyganj State Railways was taken in hand, and a subsidy of a lakh of rupees per annum guaranteed to a company who undertook to build a line between Mārgheritā and Dibrugarh. Large sums were also spent on the improvement of existing roads, the construction of bridges, and the opening out of new lines of communication.

The contract of 1887. In 1887 the Provincial share of receipts from stamps and excise was altered from 50 per cent. to 75 per cent. and 25 per cent., respectively, an arrangement which was not to the advantage of the Province. On the other hand, Assam received the whole of the land revenue, subject to the deduction of a fixed sum for Imperial needs, and half the revenue obtained under the head of assessed taxes. Grants were, moreover, made by the Supreme Government of Rs. 1,82,500 on account of capital expenditure on the Cherra-Companyganj and Jorhāt State Railways, and of Rs. 6,15,600, which represented the cost of quelling the Lushai outbreak of 1890-91. The settlement provided for an estimated expenditure of 49 lakhs of rupees per annum, and the revenues made over were calculated to bring in exactly this amount. This contract was not favourable to the Assam Administration. There was a fair expansion of revenue under land revenue and forests, but other heads showed a want of elasticity, and in some cases the average receipts fell considerably short of the estimates. The development of the Province was thus hampered by want of funds.

The contract of 1892. The settlement that came into force in 1892-93 was a consolidated one, and not a collection of separate contracts for each Provincial head. The single contribution to Imperial revenues was fixed at Rs. 11,27,000, and the whole of the land revenue receipts were at first allowed to remain Provincial, though the Supreme Government subsequently appropriated a share of the increase derived from the resettlement of the Assam Valley. During the period of this settlement Assam enjoyed considerable financial prosperity. The revenue was elastic, and no difficulty was experienced in providing for the growing wants of the Province. A special battalion of military police was organized for the Lushai Hills, and considerable sums were spent on the construction of permanent bridges and the improvement of communications.

The settlement of 1897. The chief feature of the settlement which came into force in 1897 and was extended to March 31st, 1904, was the assignment of two-thirds of the land revenue to Provincial needs. The gross ordinary expenditure of the Province was estimated at Rs. 65,29,000, and the receipts at Rs. 66,43,000, the surplus being a set-off against the necessary development of expenditure in a backward Province like Assam. The earthquake of June

12th, 1897, completely disorganized this settlement. The cost of the damage done was estimated at between 40 and 50 lakhs of rupees, and to meet this the Supreme Government made a grant of 26 lakhs. The whole resources of the Administration were devoted to the restoration of the Province to the position in which it stood prior to the earthquake, and all thought of progress had, for the time being, to be laid aside. It was, however, found possible to give effect to schemes, which had been for a long time under consideration, for the improvement of the position of the members of the Assam Commission, and of the civil police force.

The current settlement came into effect on April 1st, 1904, and will not be modified until it becomes unfair either to the Government of India or to the Province itself. Its principal features are that Assam takes one half of the revenue from land, stamps, excise, assessed taxes, forests, and registration, and is responsible for half the expenditure under these heads. The Province is also debited with the whole of the expenditure on general administration, courts of law, jails, police, medical, education, political, superannuation charges, stationery and printing, and various minor heads, receiving in its turn such revenue as is obtained from these departments. The receipts and expenditure under the heads of civil works and railways also remain Provincial, except in those cases in which railway expenditure is specially provided for from Imperial funds. An allotment of 20 lakhs of rupees was added to the balance remaining over from the former contract, and, in addition to the shares of revenue assigned, a fixed grant of 12 lakhs is annually made to the Provincial income. Further grants have since been made for the reform of the Police and Education departments. The expenditure at the commencement of the contract is estimated to amount to Rs. 72,07,000. Statistics showing the principal heads of revenue and expenditure will be found in table VIII appended to this article. The settlement of 1904.

The ordinary land tenures in Assam vary considerably in different parts of the Province, and different systems are in force in Sylhet and Goálpára, two Districts in which a large proportion of the area is permanently settled, Cáchár, Assam proper, and the hill Districts. An account of the revenue system peculiar to Cáchár, Sylhet, and Goálpára will be found in the articles on those Districts, and the following paragraphs deal only with Assam proper and the hills, and with conditions which are more or less common to the Province as a whole. LAND REVENUE.

The distinguishing features of the agricultural system of Assam proper are the large areas of unsettled waste land, and the system under which in certain tracts land is cultivated for two or three years and then resigned. These two conditions necessitate a simple system of land revenue administration, and, Assam Proper.

as a matter of fact, the ryot, provided that he pays his land revenue, is subjected to no harassing restrictions. He holds an annual or decennial lease from Government, and is free to relinquish the whole or any part of his holding, provided that notice is given to the revenue officers at the proper time. Decennial leases confer a right of resettlement and a heritable and transferable title. Annual leases merely authorise the occupation of the land covered by them for a single year, though in practice the holder can always obtain resettlement if the land is not required by Government. Any unoccupied waste land may also be taken up for cultivation without notice or application, and, when so taken up, is settled with the occupant, but a prior claim to settlement of such land may be secured by filing an application for it. Large areas of land are annually relinquished and taken up in this way in those parts of the valley where fluctuating cultivation is practised. A strong revenue staff is maintained in each District, whose principal functions are to survey and issue leases for the land newly taken up, to test the applications filed for relinquishment, to correct the revenue roll, to record the areas under different crops, and to assist in the collection of the land revenue. The country is divided into circles, as the charge of the local accountant or mandal is called, which comprise, as a rule, about 5,000 acres. Over every 20 or 25 mandals there is an officer known as a supervisor kānungo, who is continually testing their operations in the field, and supervising their work when they come in to headquarters, while above the supervisor kānungo comes the Sub-Deputy Collector, who, under the existing rules, is required to be a graduate of a University, and to have a good practical knowledge of surveying. Most of the tahsīls, or units for the collection of land revenue, are now in charge of officers of this class, and there are in addition one or two in each subdivision who are in general charge of settlement work, but have no concern with the land revenue collection.

Revenue assessment under native and British rule.

The organization of the Assamese into small bodies, or *gots* consisting of three or four individuals styled *paiks*, one of whom was always employed on the service of the state, has already been described on page 74. Each *paik* was allowed sufficient land for his homestead, and 2⅔ acres of rice land free of revenue, but was required to pay 12 annas an acre for anything taken up in excess of this quantity in addition to a poll-tax of one rupee. The revenue was farmed to *chaudhuris*, and the nominal rate assessed was only Rs. 2 a "plough," an area which, according to Buchanan Hamilton, produced about 56 cwt. of "rough rice" and 11 cwt. of mustard seed. Little control was, however, exercised over the revenue farmers, and their exactions raised the rate to about Rs. 7

per plough; while north of the Brahmaputra the demands of the hill tribes, who, with the break up of the Ahom system of administration, established a sort of right to the levy of black-mail, deprived the villagers of the whole of the profits of cultivation.

As soon as the British took possession of the country the system of forced labour was abolished, but the poll-tax was raised to Rs. 3 per head, and was subsequently commuted to a land revenue assessment. The rates varied at different times and in different portions of the valley, but in 1853 they ranged from R. 1-3-0 to 10 annas an acre of cultivated land.* In 1870, the rates per acre were fixed as follows:—Homestead, which includes the garden surrounding the house, Rs. 3; transplanted rice land R. 1-14-0; and other land R. 1-8-0. The next settlement was made in 1893 for a term of ten years. The threefold classification of land was retained, but the villages were roughly divided into four classes, and the revenue assessed on each of the three kinds of land depended upon the class in which the village fell. The main consideration taken into account in fixing the class of the village was the demand for land, as shown by the density of the population, and the proportion of settled to total area. No distinction was drawn [illegible] the good and inferior land of the same class in a village, and the assessment never pretended to anything like scientific accuracy. The rates assessed per acre were homestead Rs. 4-2-0 in first class villages to Rs. 3 in villages of the fourth class; transplanted rice land Rs. 3 to R. 1-14-0; and other land Rs. 2-4-0 to R. 1-8-0. The proportion of villages placed in the lowest class was very small, and full revenue is paid on all settled land whether cultivated or not, except in the case of land held on half rates. A detailed resettlement of two Districts, on principles similar to those which are followed in other parts of India, was commenced in 1902. The village has been abandoned as the unit of assessment, and steps are being taken to distribute the revenue more closely in accordance with the value of the actual field. A considerable area of land is held either revenue-free or at half the full rates of revenue. In 1903-04 the total settled area of Assam proper was 2,562,000 acres, the area of land held at half rates was 189,000 acres and of revenue-free land 81,000 acres. These estates represent grants made by the Ahom Rājās for religious and other purposes.

Rules for the grant of land on favourable terms.

The tea industry has played a large part in the development of Assam, and from time to time different rules have been in force to govern the grant of land for the cultivation of this plant. The earliest rules, those of 1838, applied only to Assam proper. One-fourth of the grant was to be held revenue-free in perpetuity,

---

* Report on the Province of Assam by A. J. Moffatt Mills, Calcutta, 1854, Darrang, page xiii, Lakhimpur, page 1.

and a revenue-free period of from 5 to 20 years was allowed on the remaining three-fourths, according as the land was under grass, reeds, or timber, after which light but progressive rates were imposed. The rules of 1854, which were also extended to the Surmá Valley, introduced certain modifications, but the bulk of the land taken up when they were in force was subsequently acquired in fee-simple, when the fee-simple rules were introduced in 1862. Under these rules the land was sold free of all revenue demand, the price charged varying from Rs. 2-8-0 to Rs. 10 an acre. There are now 332,000 acres of land in the Assam Valley held on this tenure. The existing rules came into force in 1876. An upset price of one rupee an acre is charged, and for two years the land is allowed to remain revenue-free. The rates gradually rise to 8 annas an acre in the eleventh and one rupee in the twenty-first year. The lease runs for 30 years, and when it expires, the land is liable to re-assessment. In the Assam Valley the issue of leases on favourable terms has never been allowed, when the land is required for the cultivation of the ordinary staples of the Province. In Cáchár this restriction was not in force, and waste land was let out at progressive rates with a revenue-free term, for ordinary as well as for special cultivation. The rules varied from time to time, but the leases were granted for 20 or thirty years, with a revenue-free period of from 2 to 3 years. The maximum revenue assessed during the concluding portion of the lease varied from 12 annas to R. 1-8-0 an acre. These rules are no longer in force, and waste land taken up for ordinary cultivation during the currency of the settlement in Cáchár is assessed at the rates levied on similar land in the neighbourhood. The ordinary form of taxation in the hill Districts is a tax of two or three rupees on each house, and no attempt is usually made to measure up the area of land actually occupied.

General considerations.

In upper Assam the villagers find a ready market for their produce in the numerous tea gardens situated in this portion of the valley, and here the assessment made in 1893 is paid without much difficulty. In lower and central Assam the tea industry is of very small importance and the people suffered severely from the earthquake of 1897 and the floods which followed it, and from the terrible mortality caused by *kalá-azár*. The Government of India accordingly directed in 1901 that the land revenue demand in this portion of the valley should be reduced by Rs. 1,80,000. Wide-spread famine or scarcity is unknown, but floods sometimes cause considerable local damage, and rules for the remission of land revenue have been introduced to afford the relief which is rendered necessary by such visitations. The area of waste land in the Province is so large that no necessity has yet arisen for checking the freedom of the ryot to transfer his land. The receipts under the head of land revenue will be found in table VIII appended to this article.

Collection of land revenue. The original system of land revenue collection in Assam was one under which an individual of some wealth and local standing, called a mauzadār, entered into a contract with Government to pay the land revenue of one or more mauzas, or fiscal divisions. The contract was formerly made for a term of years, and the mauzadār enjoyed such profits as accrued from the extension, and made good any loss due to the decrease, of cultivation, but for the last 50 years the settlement has been revised annually, and the revenue collector has been rewarded by a liberal commission which is supposed to compensate him for bad debts and other expenses. Of recent years mauzas have in many cases been grouped together to form tahsīls, in which about a lakh of rupees is realised direct from the ryots by a Government officer who receives a fixed salary, and only pays into the treasury the amount he actually collects. Difficulties have, however, been experienced in dealing direct with such large bodies of cultivators, and it has been decided gradually to abolish tahsīls, and to entrust once more the duty of collection to the mauzadār. The cost of collection is equivalent to about 5 per cent. of the demand in tahsīls and 7 per cent. in *mauzas*. If a cultivator fails to pay on the appointed date, a notice of demand is served upon him. This, as a rule, has the desired effect, but in cases of recusancy the moveable property of the defaulter, and even the land itself, can be attached and sold. The amount of revenue for which such extreme measures are taken is, however, less than one per cent. of the Government demand.

MISCELLANEOUS REVENUE.

Opium. The cultivation of opium is said to have been introduced into Assam in the reign of Lakshmī Singh, about 1770 A.D.* If this was so, the practice of opium-eating must have spread with great rapidity, as from Buchanan Hamilton's memoir it appears that in 1808 the drug was freely used by the Assamese. Consumption was unduly stimulated by the ease with which opium could be obtained, the effect upon the people was far from satisfactory, and in 1860 the cultivation of the poppy was prohibited. Supplies of opium are now received from the Board of Revenue, Bengal, and issued to licensed vendors from the Government treasuries. Opium is still largely consumed in Assam proper, and more particularly in the two Districts of Sibsāgar and Lakhimpur, which in 1903-04 took considerably more than half the total amount used in the Province; but the restrictive policy of Government has had a most marked effect upon consumption. The original duty levied in 1860 was Rs. 14 per seer, but this

* Report on the Province of Assam by A. J. Moffatt Mills. Calcutta, 1854, Sibsagar, page lxxv.

was raised by successive enhancements till in 1890 it was fixed at Rs. 37 a seer, the amount at which it now stands. In addition to raising the price of the drug, which is often sold retail for as much as 10 annas a *tola* (about 2*s.* an ounce), Government has reduced the number of shops at which it can be obtained, from 5,070 in 1873-74 to 752 in 1903-04. A further tax is placed upon the trade in the shape of license fees. Prior to 1874, licenses for retail vend were issued free of duty. In 1903-04, the amount paid to Government on account of license fees alone was no less than Rs. 3,44,000. This heavy increase in the cost of the drug, combined with an increase in the land revenue and a growing taste for imported goods, which tends to relieve the ryot of his surplus cash, has produced a remarkable decrease in consumption. In 1864-65 the total amount used in the Assam Valley was 1,939 maunds, in 1903-04 it was only 1,266 maunds. The revenue obtained from this head of excise is large, and between 1881 and 1890 averaged Rs. 16,56,000 annually, rising in the next decade to an average of Rs. 18,75,000; and in 1903-04 was Rs. 18,65,000. In addition to imposing a high rate of duty, Government attempts to restrict consumption by prohibiting the sale of more than five *tolas* ([illegible] ounces) at a time to one individual, and by forbidding the vendor to give the drug in exchange for rice or other goods.

Country spirits. The revenue from country spirits is raised on the outstill system. The sites of the shops are fixed by Government, and the right to manufacture and sell country spirits at these places is put up to auction. Local opinion is consulted before a new shop is opened, and existing stills are closed if it is shown that they offer undue temptations to the drink-consuming classes. It has, however, been proved that the mere abolition of shops does not put a stop to drinking, but merely substitutes home-made for excise liquor, and Government in its efforts to restrict consumption has constantly to bear this fact in mind. With the object of improving the excise administration, efforts are being made to introduce the central distillery system, which enables some supervision to be exercised over the quality of liquor produced. The limit of retail sale is 3 quarts, and a minimum price has been fixed of six annas a quart, except in the Khâsi Hills, where it is eight annas. Country spirits are chiefly consumed by imported coolies, and the receipts under this head are highest in those Districts in which they are most numerous. The average annual revenue rose from 2 lakhs in the period 1881-90 to 4·8 lakhs in the following decade, and in 1903-04 the receipts were 7·08 lakhs. The expansion of the revenue is due to the growth of the foreign population, and to greater vigilance and efficiency in the excise administration. The hillmen and unconverted tribes and many of the garden coolies consume large quantities of home-made rice-beer, but no attempt is made to levy duty on this liquor.

Gānja is imported from Rājshāhi under bond by warehouse keepers and is issued from their stores, on payment of duty, to the persons who have purchased the right of retail vend. The revenue has expanded *pari passu* with the growth of the foreign population; the average receipts being 2·2 lakhs between 1881 and 1890 and 3·3 lakhs in the next ten years. In 1903-04, the income under this head was 4·28 lakhs. The drug is in little favour among the Assamese, and the great bulk of the consumers are either foreigners or natives of the Surmā Valley. **Ganja.**

In comparison with other sources of revenue, the receipts from imported liquors are inconsiderable, and only amounted to Rs. 18,869 in 1903-04. The use of spirituous liquors is believed to be spreading among the more advanced sections of the native community, but the total quantity consumed by them is small, and country-made liquor still holds its own among the mass of the drinking population. The incidence of excise revenue per head of population was, *1880-81*, 6 annas 4 pies; *1890-91*, 7 annas 2 pies; *1903-04*, 8 annas 5 pies. **Imported liquors.**

The following abstract shows the average net receipts under the head of judicial and non-judicial stamps and income-tax:— **Stamps and income-tax.**

—	Average, 1881-1890 (in thousands of Rs.).	Average, 1891-1900 (in thousands of Rs.).	1903-04 (in thousands of Rs.).
Judicial stamps	5,17	6,07	7,09
Non-judicial stamps	1,97	2,33	2,74
Income-tax*	2,09	2,73	2,48

* From 1887 only.

There has been a considerable development in the stamp revenue, and this is generally considered to be an indication of the prosperity of the people, as they are only too prone to spend their surplus resources in litigation. An increase in the sale of non-judicial stamps is a sign of prosperity or the reverse, according as a recourse to borrowing is regarded as the result of the extension of trade or of straitened circumstances. The bulk of the income-tax is realised from the salaries paid to Government servants or to the managers and assistants on tea gardens. The incidence of the tax per head of population in 1903-04 was 8 pies, and the number of assessees per thousand 0·6.

LOCAL AND MUNICIPAL.

History of local self-government.

Prior to 1879, the only funds expended under local control in Assam were certain Provincial grants, and in the Districts of Sylhet and Goálpára the rates levied under the Bengal Road Cess and Zamindari Dak Acts. These allotments were managed by the District Magistrate, with the assistance, in the case of roads and education, of special road fund and education committees. In 1879, a Regulation was passed, providing for the levy of a local rate, and the appointment of a committee in each District to control the expenditure on roads, primary education, and the District post. Three years later the District committees were abolished by executive order, and their place was taken by boards established in each subdivision, which are the local authorities in existence at the present day. The Deputy Commissioner is Chairman of the board of the headquarters subdivision, but each of the other boards in the District is presided over by the Subdivisional Officer.

Powers.

The local boards are entrusted with the maintenance of all roads within their jurisdiction, except a few main lines of communication, the provision and maintenance of local staging bungalows and dispensaries, and the supervision of village sanitation, vaccination, and the District post. They are also in charge of primary education, subject to the general control of the Education department, and are empowered to make grants-in-aid to schools of higher grade, subject to certain rules. For these purposes, they have placed at their disposal the rate which is levied under the Assam Local Rates Regulation of 1879, at the rate of one anna per rupee on the annual value of lands, as well as the surplus income of pounds and ferries, and some minor receipts. This income is in most cases supplemented by an annual grant from Provincial funds, the amount of which is fixed for a term of years. The principal heads of income and expenditure are shown in table IX appended to this article. The annual budgets of the boards are submitted to the Chief Commissioner for sanction. The estimates for all works costing Rs. 500 or over must be approved by the Public Works department, and important works, requiring much professional skill, are made over for execution to that department. Less important works are entrusted to the board overseers, and in the tea Districts much assistance is usually rendered by planters in the repair of roads and bridges.

Constitution and work done.

There were in 1903-04 19 local boards in the Province consisting of 364 members, of whom 60 were *ex-officio*, 171 nominated, and 133 elected. In Districts in which the tea industry is of importance, a certain proportion of the members are planters, who are elected by the planting community. Under a system which has recently been introduced the majority of the native members will also be elected. In 1903-04, 132 members of the various boards were Europeans; and the existence of this strong European element and the comparatively small area entrusted to their charge imparts to the local boards of Assam a degree of vitality not always found in the self-governing institutions of other parts of India. Some of the largest works constructed by them during the past ten years were as follows:—Bridge over the Disai river on the Dhodar Alī in the Jorhát subdivision, cost (in round figures) Rs. 67,000; Gauripur-Rahá road in Goálpára District, cost Rs. 2,23,000; Sylhet-Muktapurghāt road in North Sylhet subdivision, cost Rs. 1,09,000; Sunámganj-Paglā road in the Sunámganj subdivision, cost Rs. 1,04,000. Large sums in the aggregate have also been spent on the improvement and repair of the existing lines of communication, the construction of bridges, wells, and roads of less importance than those already mentioned, and the maintenance of charitable dispensaries. Serious failure of the harvest occurs so seldom in Assam that local boards are hardly ever called upon to administer relief, but a small sum was distributed in Sylhet in 1902.

Only 14 urban areas in Assam are administered under some form of municipal law, and the average population of each of these places at the census of 1901 was only 6,784, ranging from 13,893 in Sylhet to 2,359 in Golághát. (Bengal) Act III of 1884 is in force in Sylhet, Gauháti, and Dibrugarh, the only towns in the Province which contain more than 10,000 inhabitants within municipal limits, and in the small town of Dhubri. The remainder are administered under (Bengal) Act V of 1876, an Act which is also in force in two "Stations" and three "Unions." The total strength of the 14 committees in 1903-04 was 141 members, 47 of whom were elected, while 70 were nominated and 24 held office *ex-officio*. Fifty of the total number were officials and 30 Europeans. The Deputy Commissioner or Subdivisional Officer is chairman of the municipality at headquarters, except in the case of the Sylhet town, but the vice-chairmen are elected by the commissioners and are usually non-officials. The little towns in Assam are often of great extent, and include semi-urban and almost rural areas. Conservancy, water-supply, and drainage are thus difficult and expensive, and the length of the roads necessitates a large expenditure, especially where metalling is involved. Generally speaking, however, a reasonable standard of efficiency is maintained. The incidence of taxation in 1903-04 was R. 1-4 per head, but the towns receive substantial grants from Government, and the average income per head was more than double this amount.

The most important public works in municipal areas are the waterworks at Gauhāti and Shillong. At Gauhāti water is pumped from the Brahmaputra to the top of a hill, and thence distributed all over the town. Since these works were completed in 1887 there has been a marked improvement in the health of the place. In Shillong the water of the hill streams is distributed in pipes over the station. Statistics showing the principal items of municipal income and expenditure will be found in table X appended to this article.

PUBLIC WORKS.

Staff.

The Public Works department in Assam is directed by a Chief or Superintending Engineer, who is also Secretary to the Chief Commissioner, aided by an Under-Secretary. The executive staff comprises twelve Executive and Assistant Engineers and two temporary Engineers. Public works in the Lushai Hills are in charge of a District-Engineer, who is an Upper Subordinate of the Public Works department, and works under the orders of the Superintendent of the Lushai Hills. The accounts of Imperial, Provincial and local works are examined and audited by an Examiner. All Provincial works, such as the construction and maintenance of the main lines of communication, and the erection and repair of all Government buildings of any size and importance are directly under the department. As has been already explained, local works involving much engineering skill are usually made over to the Executive Engineer for execution, and estimates exceeding Rs. 500 in value are submitted for professional approval.

Principal works.

The principal works completed by the department prior to 1890 were:—The south trunk road from Dhubri to Sadiyá, 456 miles, completed in 1877; the north trunk road from Dhubri to North Lakhimpur, 326 miles; metalled road from Gauháti to Shillong and from Shillong to Cherrapunji, 97 miles; road from Sylhet to Cáchár, 67 miles; road from Golághát to Nichuguard, at the foot of the Nágá Hills, 63 miles; Jorhāt State Railway, 30 miles; and Companyganj-Therriághát State Railway, 8 miles. It was originally intended to carry this line up the face of the hill to Cherrapunji, but the cost was found to be prohibitive. It was wrecked by the earthquake of 1897, and has since been abandoned.

The principal works constructed since 1890 have been the Nichuguard-Manipur road, constructed by the Imperial Government at a cost of 28¼ lakhs, and the Companyganj-Salutikar road, a section 9 miles long of the line of communication between Sylhet and Shillong. The latter runs across the line of drainage of the country, and as the rainfall in this part of the District is extremely heavy, its construction was attended with serious difficulties. The cost of the road embankment was Rs. 1,41,000; and of the bridges Rs. 1,37,000; they were, however, seriously damaged by the earthquake and by flood, and were reconstructed at a cost of Rs. 1,88,000. Considerable sums have also been spent on the Aijal-Silchar and Aijal-Lungleh roads, and the Maulavi Bazar-Manumukh road. Some of the largest bridges constructed by the

Public Works department are those over the Krishnai and Singrā rivers on the south trunk road, and over the Digru between Shillong and Gauhāti. The cost of each was between three-quarters of a lakh and a lakh of rupees. Since 1897, the resources of the Province have been largely devoted to the restoration of buildings destroyed by the earthquake. The most expensive have been:—The Secretariat Press, cost Rs. 1,27,000; Government House, Shillong, cost Rs. 1,91,000; Sylhet Collectorate, cost 1,68,000, and Sylhet Jail, cost Rs. 1,86,000. Other important works have been the Aijal waterworks, cost Rs. 1,36,000, and the Manipur cantonments, estimate Rs. 6,56,000.

ARMY.

Assam is comprised in the Lucknow division of the Eastern Command. The military stations are at present (1904) Dibrugarh, Kohīmā, Manipur, Sadiyá, and Shillong. The total strength of the British and Native army stationed within the Province on 1st June 1903 was 2,227, of whom 58 were British.

There are volunteer corps with headquarters at Silchar, Dibrugarh, Lumding and Shillong, and their strength in 1903 was 731, of whom 637 were light horse or mounted rifles. In the Assam Valley separate volunteer corps were originally started in each district, the first to be enrolled being the Lakhimpur corps in 1882. In 1891, the mounted infantry in the four upper Districts of the valley were formed into one corps under the designation of the Assam Valley Mounted Rifles, and five years later were converted into a body of light horse, which in 1903-04 had an efficient strength of 349. A volunteer corps was started in Sylhet in 1880 and in Cáchár in 1883, and the two were subsequently amalgamated into the Surmá Valley Light Horse, which in 1903-04 had an efficient strength of 270.

POLICE AN JAILS.

Police.

The police force of the Province consists of civil police, rural police or village chaukīdārs, and military police. Under native rule there seems to have been little or no police administration, as we understand the term, and even in 1853 the total force employed in the Assam Valley was only 547 men. The numbers were, however, rapidly increased, and in 1874, when Assam was separated from Bengal, the civil police consisted of 3,452 persons. The development of the military police rendered it possible to reduce the other arm of the force, which in 1903 consisted of 383 officers and 2,289 men, allowing one policeman engaged on the prevention and detection of crime to every 20 square miles, and every 2,185 people. The corresponding figures for rural police in the three Districts in which alone they are employed were 2 and 458 respectively. The present sanctioned scale of superior officers is six District Superintendents of Police and eleven Assistant Superintendents. Under the revised scale there will be ten of the former and five of the latter.

Recruitment and training.

For ordinary constables strong young men between 18 and 25, who are able to read and write, are selected as recruits. If required for the armed police, the selection is generally restricted to up-countrymen or to members of the aboriginal tribes. Appointments to the grade of sub-inspector are occasionally made from the rank and file of the force, but the usual procedure is to select probationers from the list of approved candidates, who are drawn from a superior social position. Head constables and constables are trained by their immediate superiors; probationary sub-inspectors are placed under the orders of a selected inspector, and are not confirmed until a satisfactory report has been received of their conduct and capacity. The rural policeman is required to report all serious crime to the officer in charge of the police station within which his village is situated, to arrest persons committing such crimes in his presence, to collect vital statistics, to observe the movement of bad characters, and generally to inform his official superiors of anything likely to affect the peace and good administration of the District. Rural police are not employed in Assam proper, as there is little serious crime in that portion of the Province, and the gaonbura, or village elder, gives such assistance as is necessary. Educated natives used formerly to object to taking service in the department. The position and the moral tone of the police have, however, been improved of recent years, and the competition for ministerial appointments is so keen that young men of good family are glad to accept nominations to the sub-inspector grade. The pay of the ordinary constable is not, however, sufficient to attract or retain a good class of recruit, and the readiness with which the men resign is a serious obstacle to the efficient management of the force.

A system of anthropometry was introduced into Assam in 1893, but was superseded in 1898 by the system of identification from finger prints. The civil police are at present armed with smooth-bore snider carbines, but bored-out Martini-Henry rifles will shortly be issued in their place. The strength of the civil and military police force is shown in detail in table XI.

Military Police

Prior to 1878, there were three separate bodies of *quasi*-military police in the Nágá and Gáro Hills and in the Surmā Valley, but in 1878 the frontier police were formed into a separate force, and detachments stationed in each District. In 1882, the Assam Military Police Regulation came into force, and in 1903 the force consisted of five battalions, with an actual strength of 2,863 officers and men. The headquarters of the battalions are at Aijal in the Lushai Hills, Silchar, Kohīmá in the Nágá Hills, Turá in the Gáro Hills, and Dibrugarh; but during the cold weather the military police hold 36 different outposts, the majority of which are intended to keep in check the hill tribes on our frontier. The force has recently been re-armed with Martini-Henry rifles, and the officers commanding the four battalions at Silchar, Aijal, Kohīmā, and Dibrugarh are all military men. The military police form a valuable fighting force, and have taken part in the Manipur, Lushai, Abor, Apa Tanang, and Mishmi expeditions, where they served with great credit. Railway police are only employed on the Assam-Bengal Railway and the Jorhāt State Railway. The total strength on the whole of these two lines consists of 3 officers and 51 head constables and men. The average number of cases in the five years ending 1901 may be classified as follows:—Investigated 9,971; tried in court 5,251; ending in acquittal or discharge 993; ending in conviction 4,052.

Jails.

The jails at Shillong and at the headquarters of six plains Districts are classed as District jails, as distinguished from the subsidiary jails at all the plains subdivisions except Hailākāndi and Barpetā, and at Dhubri, Nowgong, Kohīmā, Turā, and Aijal. Of the former class, there were 7 in 1903, of the latter 17. The largest jails are those at SYLHET, which had a daily average population of 414, TEZPUR, daily average 210, GAUHATI, daily average 249, and DIBRUGARH, daily average 110. European prisoners can be confined in these jails, provided that the term of imprisonment does not exceed one month. Prisoners are not, as a rule, confined for more than six months in subsidiary jails, and convicts sentenced to longer terms are generally transferred to the District jail. The jail mortality has usually been high in Assam Valley, but in this respect it has not differed from that which prevails in the Province as a whole. The most prevalent diseases are dysentery, diarrhœa, and fever, and there are occasional outbreaks of cholera. The jail industries are not of great importance. They include the making of cane and basket-work furniture, the weaving of prison clothing and rough cloth, rice-husking, pressing of mustard oil, and gardening. At one time prisoners were largely employed on extramural labour, but this system has been, to a great extent, abandoned of recent years, as it tends to a relaxation of discipline. The larger jails are in charge of the civil medical officers of the Districts in which they are situated. The salient statistics with regard to the jails of the Province are shown in table XII.

EDUCATION.
Early history.

Under native rule very little attention was paid to education, and it is said that in 1838 there were barely 30 educated people in the District of Nowgong.* The Province was subsequently incorporated in the charge of an Inspector, Mr. Robinson, who in 1841 reported† that the state of education in the Brahmaputra valley was "deplorable in the extreme," while fifteen years later he calculated that in the whole of his division, which included several Districts of Bengal, there were only 13,300 boys under

* Report on the Province of Assam, by A. J. Moffatt Mills, Calcutta, 1854, page 26.
† A Descriptive Account of Assam, by W. Robinson, Calcutta, 1841, page 277.

tuition out of 1,262,000 children of school-going age. By 1856 English schools had been established in Sylhet and Gauháti, 7 Anglo-vernacular schools in Sylhet, all of which were closed in the following year, 3 in Cāchár, and 1 in Goálpára, and a Government vernacular school at the headquarters of each of the five Districts of Assam proper. In the Brahmaputra Valley these were supplemented by schools in the villages, which had nearly 4,000 pupils, though the system of tuition was far from satisfactory, but even as late as 1868 less than 1,500 children were under instruction in the Surmá Valley,* though the total population must have been about two million. The earliest year for which it is possible to obtain statistics for the Province as a whole is 1875. By that time the system initiated by Sir George Campbell of encouraging indigenous institutions by the offer of grants-in-aid had begun to take effect, and the number of schools had risen to 1,193 and of scholars to 30,000. In 1903-04, 106,000 persons were under instruction, and 3,232 educational institutions existed. The department is now under the control of a Director of Public Instruction, an officer who is recruited from England, and is assisted by a staff of Inspectors, Deputy Inspectors, and Sub-Inspectors of Schools.

College education. After the closing of college classes at Gauháti in 1876 the Province was without any form of University education, and to meet this defect 36 scholarships for sums varying from Rs. 25 to Rs. 10 per mensem were allotted to boys who passed the Entrance examination with most credit. These scholarships were tenable for two years at any of the affiliated colleges in Bengal, and were extended for a further like period if the holders passed the First Arts examination satisfactorily. In 1892, the Murāri Chand second-grade unaided college was opened at Sylhet. It was founded and is maintained by a zamīndār of that District, Rājā Girish Chandra Roy, and teaches up to the First Arts standard, the full college course occupying two years. In 1901, a Government second-grade college was opened at Gauháti. The buildings have been designed on liberal lines, and include an excellent library and laboratory, and separate hostels for Hindus and Muhammadans. No institution in the Province confers degrees, but during the 12 years ending 1900 the degree of B.A. of the Calcutta University was obtained by 68 natives of the Surmā Valley, 29 of the Brahmaputra Valley, and 2 of the hill Districts. In the same period 21 persons educated in Assam obtained the M.A. degree.

* Principal Heads of the History and Statistics of the Dacca Division, Calcutta, 1868, pages 326 and 365.

Secondary education is imparted in high and middle schools, which are again subdivided into middle English and middle vernacular. High schools are those institutions which are recognised by the Calcutta University as capable of affording suitable preparation for the Entrance examination. The boys are taught from the earliest stage of their education up to the Entrance course as prescribed by the University of Calcutta, but many leave school without completing the course. Till recently English was taught in all the classes. The smaller boys no longer learn that language, but the standard of instruction is higher than that prevailing in lower secondary (middle) schools. English is the medium of instruction in the first four classes of high schools; in the lower classes and in other schools the vernacular is employed. In 1903-04, 10 high schools in the Province were under Government management, 9 were aided, that is to say, private institutions towards which Government makes a fixed contribution, and 7 were unaided schools. The course of instruction at middle English and middle vernacular schools is the same, with the exception that English is taught in the former and not in the latter. The following are the subjects taught in the middle vernacular course:—Bengali or Assamese, comprising literature, grammar and composition, history of India, geography, arithmetic, Euclid (Book I), mensuration of plane surfaces and surveying, and elementary natural and sanitary science. In 1903-04, there were 75 middle English and 42 middle vernacular schools for boys. Of the middle schools, 78 were under private management, but received grants from Government or local and municipal funds. Eighteen were entirely unaided. Grants are only made to those schools which meet a recognised want, and are likely to be properly maintained, and do not, as a rule, exceed the amount provided for the school from fees and other sources. Three per cent. of the male population of school-going age were under secondary instruction in 1903-04. **Secondary education.**

Primary education is again divided into upper and lower, but the proportion of boys in upper primary schools is less than five per cent. of the total number, and this class of school, like the middle vernacular, is slowly dying out. The course of study in lower primary schools includes reading, writing, dictation, simple arithmetic, and the geography of Assam, but in 1903-04, 60 per cent. of the pupils were classed as illiterate, as they were unable to read and write. In upper primary schools the course is somewhat more advanced, and includes part of the first book of Euclid, mensuration, and a little history. Primary schools are usually managed by local boards or municipalities, and very few are managed by Government. The standard of instruction given still leaves much to be desired, but efforts have been recently made to improve **Primary education.**

it, by raising the rates of pay given to the masters. Fixed pay is now awarded at average rates of Rs. 8 per mensem for certificated and Rs. 5 per mensem for uncertificated teachers, supplemented by capitation grants at rates ranging from 3 annas to 6 annas for pupils in the three highest classes. Under the system formerly in force rewards were granted on the results of examinations, and there was thus some risk that the master might concentrate his attention on his brighter pupils and neglect the more backward scholars. These examinations have in consequence been abolished, except in so far as they are required for the grant of scholarships. Seventeen per cent. of the boys of school-going age were under primary instruction in 1903-04. The largest proportion of boys of school-going age attending school is found in the Khási and Jaintiā Hills, where in 1903-04 it was 33 per cent. Kámrūp (29 per cent.) had the highest proportion in the plains, and in Darrang and Lakhimpur it was less than 17 per cent.

Female education.

Altogether 150 girls' schools were maintained in the Province in 1903-04, the proportion of girls actually under instruction to those of school-going age being 15 per mille, as compared with 12 and 5 in 1891 and 1881. The majority of the schools were of the lower primary class, and were thus under the management of the local boards, but in the Khāsi Hills there is a good secondary school maintained by the Welsh Mission, and the success that has attended their efforts can be judged from the fact that in 1901, 34 per mille of the female population of the District were returned as literate, as compared with 4 per mille in the Province as a whole. Elsewhere, the children are withdrawn from school before they have time to make much progress, and the condition of female education cannot be considered satisfactory. The subjects taught include sewing, in addition to those prescribed for the ordinary lower primary course. In the Khási and Jaintiá Hills 15 per cent. of the girls of school-going age attended school in 1903-04, but in the plains no District had a larger proportion than Goālpāra, and there it was only 1 per cent.

Special schools.

The only forms of special schools in the Province are those for training teachers, a medical and an engineering school, and law classes. Only two training schools are now maintained, and arrangements have been made to train teachers at selected secondary schools. A medical school was established at Dibrugarh in 1900 with the help of a legacy left by the late Brigade-Surgeon Berry-White. It is maintained by Government, and teaches up to the civil hospital assistant standard, the course occupying four years. There were 101 students on its rolls in 1903-04. The engineering school, at Dibrugarh is maintained from the proceeds of a fund left by the late Mr. Williamson, a tea planter of the Sibságar District. The school teaches up to the sub-overseer standard, but its working has not been satisfactory, and it has been decided to close it and to devote the funds thus set free to the establishment of scholarships tenable at an efficient engineering college elsewhere. Law classes are held at Gauháti, Sibságar, Sylhet and Silchar.

European education. The only educational institution for European and Eurasian children in the Province is the middle school at Shillong. It was opened in 1881, closed after the earthquake of 1897, which destroyed the building, and reopened three years later. The number of pupils on the rolls in 1903-04 was 29.

Muhammadan education. Muhammadans are not as fully alive to the advantages of education as Hindus, and in 1901 the proportion of literate persons among them was less than half that prevailing among the Hindus. This is partly due to the fact that the immense majority of the upper and middle classes are Hindus, Islām obtaining most of its converts in Assam from the lower Hindu castes. The proportion of Muhammadans in high schools is barely a third of that of Hindus, and in middle and primary schools it is little over one-half. Special consideration is given to the claims of educated Muhammadans when making appointments to Government service, and efforts have been made to improve the character of instruction in their private schools.

General educational results. The gradual spread of education in the earlier days of British rule has been already referred to, and the proportion of children under instruction to those of a school-going age rose from 57 per thousand in 1880-81 to 90 in 1890-91, and to 121 in 1903-04. According to the census of 1901, 36 persons per thousand were able to read and write. Education has made most progress in the Surmá Valley, and in the Cáchár plains 91 and in Sylhet 81 out of every thousand males were classed as literate. In the valley of the Brahmaputra the ratio varied from 68 in Kámrūp to 49 in Goálpára. The proportion in the hill Districts was 50, but this high rate is partly due to the presence of a considerable foreign literate population in the hills. Except among the Khásis, the number of women who could read and write was inconsiderable. The best educated sections of the community are the higher Hindu castes, such as the Brāhman, Kāyasth, Ganak and Baidya. A considerable proportion of native Christians and Sháhás are also literate, but few of the aboriginal tribes, except the Khásis, Gāros, and Lushais, have mastered even the elements, though schools have in many cases been opened for their special benefit. The fees charged can hardly be considered prohibitive. In the upper classes of high schools boys pay from Rs. 2 to Rs. 3 per mensem, but education in lower primary schools is free, though presents are sometimes made to the teachers.

Educational finance.

The following table shows the direct expenditure incurred on various grades of schools in 1903-04 :—

—	Expenditure on institutions maintained or aided by public funds in 1903-04 from				
	Provincial Revenues.	District and municipal funds.	Fees.	Other sources.	Total.
	Rs.	Rs.	Rs.	Rs.	Rs.
Arts Colleges ...	8,496*	...	6,604	3,464	18,564
Training and special schools	28,560	5,714	5,159	9,738	49,171
Secondary boys' schools ...	37,983	33,273	1,32,108	36,881	2,40,245
Primary ditto ...	16,525	2,14,015	20,222	60,883	3,11,645
Girls' schools	4,604	10,968	1,135	5,797	22,504
Total	96,168	2,63,970	1,65,228	1,16,763	6,42,129

Newspapers and books.

In 1903-04, 9 papers were published in Assam, of which 3 were in English, 2 in Bengali, 1 in Assamese, and 3 in Khási. None of these papers was issued oftener than once a week, and not one had as many as 1,200 subscribers, the average circulation being about 750. Only 9 books were published in 1903-04, most of which were small treatises of an educational character or works on religious subjects.

MEDICAL.

There are no large medical institutions in the Province, but 135 dispensaries are maintained, of which 35 have accommodation for in-patients. The largest hospitals are those at Dibrugarh (98 beds), Dhubri (37 beds), Tezpur (40 beds), and Nowgong (38 beds). One of these institutions has been opened at the headquarters of each District and subdivision, and of recent years there has been a large increase in the number of rural or village dispensaries. The marked development in the number of dispensaries and in the extent to which they have been used by the people during the last twenty-three years is shown in the following abstract :—

	1881.	1891.	1901.	1903.
Number of civil hospitals and dispensaries	25	74	125	127
Average daily number of in-door patients	161	212	361	374
" " out-door patients...	448	1,490	3,460	3,829
	Rs.	Rs.	Rs.	Rs.
Income from—				
(a) Government payments ...	16,105	35,237	75,371	81,788
(b) Local and municipal payments	8,593	52,278	94,964	94,259
(c) Fees, endowments, and other sources ...	15,007	51,562	85,257	81,511
Expenditure on—				
(a) Establishment ...	18,026	45,054	84,475	96,069
(b) Medicines, diet, buildings, etc.	19,516	92,020	1,67,539	1,11,675

Between 1881 and 1901 the population of the Province increased by 19 per cent., but the number of cases treated in 1903 was nearly sixteen times that of the number in 1881, and more than eight operations were performed for every one carried out in the earlier year. The mass of the people in the Assam Valley are, however, still indifferent to the advantages to be obtained from European methods. The majority of cases treated at the dispensaries are of a very simple character, and the operations performed are for the most part unimportant. A leper asylum has recently been opened at Sylhet. The total number of lepers treated in 1903 was 48.

There is an asylum at Tezpur, to which insane persons are sent from the hill Districts and the Assam Valley. Lunatics from the Surmá Valley are sent to the Dacca asylum.

The salient statistics of the Tezpur asylum are shown in the following abstract :—

	1881.	1891.	1901.	1903.
Average daily number of—				
(a) Criminal lunatics ...	18	30	37	54
(b) Other lunatics	34	90	82	101
	Rs.	Rs.	Rs.	Rs.
Income from—				
(a) Government payments ...	7,454	8,729	12,761	14,987
(b) Fees and other sources ...	600	150	1,672	686
Expenditure on—				
(a) Establishment	3,786	3,973	4,499	5,265
(b) Diet, buildings, etc. ...	4,268	5,564	8,922	10,479

In the ten years ending with 1901 there were 350 admissions. In 232 cases the cause of insanity was unknown, in 45 cases *gānja* was said to have been the predisposing cause, in 16 epilepsy, in 12 fever, in 10 spirit drinking, in 9 heredity, and in 6 opium.

Vaccination.

Inoculation is still practised in different parts of the Province. The virus is obtained from persons whose small-pox eruptions are about eight days old, and after it has been diluted with water it is applied to small incisions which have been made in the arm of the patient. An attack of small-pox supervenes, and if the patient recovers, his chances of contracting the disease in the ordinary way are very slight. Unfortunately, in many cases the person inoculated dies, and under any circumstances he is a dangerous source of infection to his neighbours. Inoculators seldom take service in the vaccination department, though preference is given to them before other candidates.

Vaccination is only compulsory in the larger towns, which in 1901 had a population of 79,845, but, except among the Mahāpurushias, a somewhat bigoted sect of Vaishnavites, whose headquarters are at Barpetá in Kāmrūp, its advantages are generally recognised. In 1903, 263 vaccinators were entertained. Further information is given in the following abstract:—

	1880-81.	1890-91.	1900-01.	1903-04.
Population among whom vaccination was carried on	*	5,422,745	6,126,343	6,126,343
Number of successful operations ...	21,170	161,157	257,336	271,295
Ratio per thousand of population ...	*	27	42	44
		Rs. a. p.	Rs. a. p.	Rs. a. p.
Total expenditure on vaccination	*	15,841 0 0	22,833 0 0	24,381 0 0
Cost per successful case ...	*	0 1 9	0 1 8	0 1 9

Sale of quinine.

The system of selling pice packets of quinine at post offices was first brought into full working in 1896. In that year 67,000 packets were sold through the agency of the postal department and 33,000 by missionaries in the Khási and Jaintiá Hills. In 1903-04 the number of packets sold was 105,000 but, in 1898, which was a very unhealthy year, more than double this quantity was disposed of.

Rural sanitation.

The sanitation of rural areas is in a far from satisfactory condition. There are no conservancy arrangements, and the water supply is usually drawn from sluggish rivers and tanks exposed to every form of pollution, or from shallow wells. A considerable number of masonry wells have been constructed at central sites

* Information not available.

by the local authorities, but unfortunately the Assamese often decline to use them. In 1896, a system of sanitary inspection books was inaugurated in 110 villages, but it is doubtful whether any practical advantages have accrued. In the hills the villages are, as a rule, built on sites which are fairly free from jungle, and, though often very dirty, are exposed to the purifying influences of the sun and air.

The following account of the surveys of the Province is taken from the General Administration Report for the year 1902-03:— SURVEYS.
"The professional revenue survey of the plains Districts of the Province was undertaken while these Districts formed part of Bengal, and was brought to a conclusion shortly after the formation of the Chief Commissionership. In this survey village boundaries, where they existed, and the boundaries of certain tea grants and revenue-free estates, as well as the geographical and topographical features of the country, were mapped, usually on the scale of 4 inches to a mile; but, except in the Jaintiá Parganas and Cáchár, no field survey was made, and the results were of little practical use for revenue purposes. In the permanently settled portion of Sylhet, the survey was preceded in the years 1859-65 by a demarcation of the boundaries of villages and estates by non-professional agency, in the course of which maps of the estates were prepared by chain and compass on the scale of 16 inches to a mile, and these maps, inaccurate though they are in many respects, afford the most recent record of the boundaries of estates in that area. A cadastral survey, based on a regular professional traverse of the portions of the Assam Valley where most cultivation was to be found, was commenced in 1883 and completed in 1893, and similar cadastral surveys of the *ryotwāri* portions of Sylhet and Cáchár have been effected for resettlement purposes in subsequent years. The field maps of these surveys are on the scale of 16 inches to a mile. While the cadastral survey of a portion of the Assam Valley Districts was in progress, the opportunity was taken to train the local mandals in surveying with the plane table, and after the professional party had left the valley, certain additional areas were surveyed cadastrally by local agency on the basis of plane-table traverses in successive years. It was subsequently decided that all such extension surveys should be made on the basis of theodolite traverses, and since 1899 a permanent professional survey detachment has been maintained in the Province, which is charged with the duty of preparing traverses for further cadastral survey which the extension of cultivation may necessitate, as well as with correcting and bringing up to date the topographical details in the standard District maps, and with minor survey operations undertaken in the Province which require professional skill. Wherever an area has been brought under cadastral survey,

arrangements have been made for having the maps and other records kept as far as possible up to date, and the permanent marks looked after by the agency of mandals in the Brahmaputra valley and patwāris in the Surmá Valley. The Gáro, Khási and Jaiñtiā, and Nágá Hills, and a portion of the Lushai Hills have been surveyed by the Topographical Branch of the Imperial Survey Department."

Bibliography. A full bibliography of writings dealing with Assam will be found in the *Report on the Progress of Historical Research in Assam*, (Shillong), 1897. Other authorities which may be consulted are W. Robinson, *A Descriptive Account of Assam*, 1841; *Principal Heads of the History and Statistics of the Dacca Division*, (Calcutta), 1868; A. J. Moffatt Mills, *Report on the Province of Assam*, (Calcutta), 1854; Sir W. W. Hunter, *A Statistical Account of Assam*, 1879; J. M'Cosh, *Topography of Assam*, (Calcutta), 1837; A. Mackenzie, *History of the relations of the Government with the Hill Tribes of the North-East Frontier of Bengal*, (Calcutta), 1884; R. B. Pemberton, *Report on the Eastern Frontier of British India*, (Calcutta), 1835; *Census of Assam, 1881, 1891, and 1901*; *Introduction to the Land Revenue Manual, Assam*, (Calcutta), 1896; *An Account of the Province of Assam and its Administration*, (Shillong), 1903; *Various papers in the Journal of the Asiatic Society of Bengal*, more particularly Volume XLI, Part I, *Assam in the 16th and 17th Centuries*, by H. Blochman; and Volume LXII, Part I, No. 4; E. A. Gait, *the Koch Kings of Kamarupa*, (Shillong), 1895; *a History of Assam*, by E. A. Gait; and a series of district Gazetteers by B. C. Allen are under publication.

TABLE I.

Temperature in Assam.

Station.	Height of observatory above sea-level.	Average temperature for 25 years ending with 1901 in							
		January.		May.		July.		November.	
		Mean.	Diurnal Range.*	Mean.	Diurnal Range.*	Mean.	Diurnal Range.*	Mean.	Diurnal Range.*
	Feet.								
Silchar ...	104	65·0	25·3	80·6	16·1	83·7	12·9	74·3	21·3
Sibsaga ...	333	59·9	20·1	78·7	14·4	84·0	12·0	69·0	18·3
Dhubri† ...	115	63·4	20·4	77·5	9·0	80·4	4·0	71·8	16·5

* Average difference between maximum and minimum temperatures of each day.
† The figures for January are an average of 20 years and the other of 21.

TABLE II.

Rainfall in Assam.

Station.	Average rainfall (in inches) for 25 years ending with 1901 in												Total of year.
	January.	February.	March.	April.	May.	June.	July.	August.	September.	October.	November.	December.	
Silchar ...	0·71	1·87	8·35	14·51	16·57	21·47	18·79	19·92	14·14	5·84	1·58	0·57	124·32
Sibsagar ...	1·24	1·83	4·88	9·15	12·02	13·58	16·41	15·91	12·36	5·22	0·99	0·61	94·20
Dhubri* ...	0·43	0·60	1·95	4·65	15·02	24·30	16·47	12·78	13·85	3·29	0·29	0·14	93·77

* The figures for October to December are for 24 years.

TABLE III.

Distribution of Population, Assam, 1901.

Natural or administrative divisions.	Area, in square miles.	Number of towns.	Number of villages.	Total population.			Urban population.			Persons per square mile in rural areas.
				Persons.	Males.	Females.	Persons.	Males.	Females.	
Surmá Valley.										
Cáchár	3,769	1	1,332	455,593	244,161	211,432	9,256	6,575	2,681	119
Sylhet	5,388(c)	5	8,330	2,241,848	1,141,060	1,100,788	30,832	19,046	11,786	410
Total Surmá Valley...	9,157	6	9,662	2,697,441	1,385,221	1,312,220	40,088	25,621	14,467	291
Brahmaputra Valley.										
Goálpára ...	3,961	2	1,461	462,052	242,685	219,367	10,024	6,868	3,156	114
Kámrúp ...	3,858	2	1,716	589,187	292,869	296,318	20,408	11,993	8,415	147
Darrang ...	3,418	1	1,275	337,313	176,030	161,283	5,047	3,568	1,479	97
Nowgong ...	3,843	1	1,117	261,160	132,995	128,165	4,430	2,659	1,771	67
Sibságar ...	4,996	3	2,109	597,969	316,985	280,984	10,970	6,660	4,310	118
Lakhimpur ...	4,529(c)	1	1,123	371,396	199,359	172,037	11,227	7,091	4,136	84
Total Brahmaputra valley.	24,605	10	8,801	2,619,077	1,360,923	1,258,154	62,106	38,839	23,267	104

Hill Districts.										
Lushai Hills ...	7,227	...	239	82,434	39,004	43,430	...	...	...	11
Nágá ,, ...	3,070	1	292	102,402	51,656	50,746	3,093	2,174	919	32
Khási and Jaintiá Hills.	6,027	1	1,839	202,250	97,221	105,029	8,384	4,980	3,404	32
Gáro Hills ...	3,140	...	1,026	138,274	70,035	68,239	...	...	...	44
Total Hill Districts...	19,464	2	3,396	525,360	257,916	267,444	11,477	7,154	4,323	26
Total British territory.	53,226	18	21,859	5,841,878	3,004,060	2,837,818	113,671	71,614	42,057	108
Manipur State ...	8,456(c)	1	467	284,465	139,632	144,833	67,093	32,965	34,128	34(a)
Grand Total ...	61,682	19	22,326	6,126,343	3,143,692	2,982,651	180,764	104,579	76,185	97(b)

(a) For total area of State.

(b) The total area and population of Manipur have been taken as rural.

(c) Area modified since publication of Census Report of 1901.

TABLE IV.

Statistics of agriculture in the Assam Valley Division, excluding the permanently-settled estates in Goalpara.

—	Average for 7 years ending 1889-90.	Average for 10 years ending 1899-00.	1900-01.	1903-04.
	Acres.	Acres.	Acres.	Acres.
Current fallow ...	*	586,358	785,582	791,340
Unsettled waste ...	*	8,159,488	9,376,605	9,642,130
Rice	1,164,286	1,287,917	1,235,190	1,380,410
Other food grains, including pulses.	55,075	66,542	65,053	74,545
Oil-seeds	154,718	164,323	123,406	161,764
Sugarcane	18,591	17,451	17,937	19,388
Tea	113,914	159,701	204,955	204,702
Miscellaneous	197,304	238,546	219,792	199,830
Total area cropped ...	1,703,888	1,934,480	1,866,333	2,040,639
Area double cropped ...	175,304	180,014	134,687	181,225
Net area cropped ...	1,528,584	1,754,466	1,731,646	1,859,414

* Figures not available.

TABLE V.

Statistics of prices of food staples in seers per rupee, Assam.

Articles.	Cachar.				Sylhet.				Kamrup.				Lakhimpur.			
	Average for 10 years ending			Year 1903.	Average for 10 years ending			Year 1903.	Average for 10 years ending			Year 1903.	Average for 10 years ending			Year 1903.
	1880.	1890.	1900.		1880.	1890.	1900.		1880.	1890.	1900.		1880.	1890.	1900.	
Common rice	19	17	12	15	21	20	13	14	16	17	13	13	11	13	11	10
Wheat ...	10(*a*)	10	8	8	12	12	12(*b*)	...	15	14	8	8	9	9	7	8
Gram ...	13	14(*a*)	11	12	15	16(*a*)	11	13	10	13	11	12	9	12(*a*)	10	11
Salt ...	8	10	9	12	9	11	10	12	8	10	10	11	6	9	8	9

(*a*) Average for 9 years.

(*b*) Figures for one year only, ten years' figures not available.

TABLE VI.

PART I.

Statistics of the value in rupees (thousands omitted) of the Rail and River-borne Trade of Assam with the other Provinces of India for the official years 1890-91, 1900-01, *and* 1903-04.

Articles.	1890-91.	1900-01.	1903-04.
Imports, Foreign and Indian goods—			
Cotton, twist and yarn ...	9,55	9,08	9,08
" piece-goods	86,77	86,66	89,56
Gram and pulse	9,72	13,84	14,25
Metals	27,14	39,68	28,83
Oils, kerosene	9,39	11,71	10,38
" others...	12,17	21,41	14,09
Rice not in the husk	6,15	38,41	19,87
Salt	20,55	20,65	14,45
Sugar	19,24	22,14	28,10
Tobacco	8,84	13,97	12,61
All other articles	61,58	1,25,50	1,31,68
Total	2,71,10	4,03,05	3,72,90
Exports—			
Caoutchouc...	3,63	3,82	1,18
Coal and coke	10,58	9,50	15,49
Cotton, raw	1,52	3,21	3,14
Hides and skins	2,17	5,65	9,32
Jute	8,52	15,10	17,99
Lac	1,13	1,99	4,92
Oil-seeds	36,08	25,90	35,51
Oranges	2,30	1,21	13,58
Rice in the husk	32,74	31,36	42,18
Stone and lime	6,83	6,51	2,91
Tea	3,39,74	4,46,66	5,51,81
Wood	...	14,99	16,57
All other articles	88,24	68,75	51,00
Total	4,83,48	6,34,65	7,65,60

TABLE VI.

PART II.

Statistics of the value in rupees (thousands omitted) of the foreign land trade of Assam for the official years 1890-91, 1900-01, *and* 1903-04.

(*N.B.*—This table does not include trade with Manipur or Hill Tippera.)

Articles.	1890-91.	1900-01.	1903-04.
Imports—			
Blankets	8	5	7
Horses and ponies	23	15	85
Rubber	1,00	1,82	1,57
Spices	4	6	12
Wax	6	11	27
All other articles	23	26	1,30
Total	1,64	2,45	4,18
Exports—			
Cotton, twist and yarn	2	4	9
Cotton, piece-goods	2	9	8
Opium	7	...	...
Rice, husked	10	7	4
Salt	3	4	3
Silk	19	36	56
All other articles	17	17	34
Total	60	77	1,14

TABLE VII.

Statistics of Criminal Justice in the plains Districts of Assam.

—	Average for 10 years ending 1890.	Average for 10 years ending 1900.	1901.	1903.	Percentage of convictions in 1903.
Number of persons tried—					
(a) For offences against person and property.	9,610	10,807	11,273	11,573	37
(b) For other offences against the Indian Penal Code.	2,851	3,821	3,589	3,327	55
(c) For offences against Special and Local Laws.	4,616	7,762	6,654	7,343	63
Total	17,077	22,390	21,516	22,243	48

Statistics of Civil Justice in the plains Districts of Assam.

—	Average for 10 years ending 1890.	Average for 10 years ending 1900.	1901.	1903.
Suits for money and moveable property.	20,409	19,532	20,684	21,121
Title and other suits ...	2,514	3,577	3,220	4,076
Rent suits	1,972	3,811	4,966	4,836
Total	24,895	26,920	28,870	30,033

TABLE VIII.

A.

Principal sources of ordinary Provincial revenue in rupees Assam, (thousands omitted).

—	Average for 10 years ending 31st March 1890.		Average for 10 years ending 31st March 1900.		Year ending 31st March 1901.		Year ending 31st March 1904.	
	Total amount raised (Imperial, Provincial, and Local).	Amount credited to Provincial revenues.	Total amount raised (Imperial, Provincial, and Local).	Amount credited to Provincial revenues.	Total amount raised (Imperial, Provincial, and Local).	Amount credited to Provincial revenues.	Total amount raised (Imperial, Provincial, and Local).	Amount credited to Provincial revenues.
Land revenue ...	41,13	24,06	56,13	43,37	62,15	46,75	63,68	67,51
Stamps ...	7,35	4,89	8,62	6,47	9,47	7,10	9,87	7,41
Excise ...	21,16	10,86	27,17	6,79	29,34	7,33	30,24	7,56
Assessed taxes ...	2,18(a)	1,09(a)	2,76	1,38	2,98	1,49	2,48	1,2
Forests ...	2,50(b)	1,25(b)	4,18	2,09	5,50	2,75	6,76	3,3
Registration ...	34	20	48	24	56	28	70	3
Other sources ...	10,44	5,33	13,42	5,64	28,01	5,34	37,79	5,5
Total ...	83,07	46,66	1,12,76	65,98	1,38,01	71,04	1,51,52	93,02

(a) The average is for 8 years. | (b) The average is for 8 years.

TABLE VIII.

B.

Provincial expenditure under principal heads in rupees, Assam, (thousands omitted).

—	Average for 10 years ending 31st March 1890.	Average for 10 years ending 31st March 1900.	Year ending 31st March 1901.	Year ending 31st March 1904.
Opening balance ...	8,87	11,13	5,40	16,09
1. Charges in respect of collection (principally Land Revenue and Forests).	8,82	11,71	12,09	13,05
2. Salaries and Expenses of Civil Departments—				
(a) General Administration.	1,93	2,68	2,94	3,38
(b) Law and Justice ...	6,15	6,81	7,52	8,77
(c) Police	9,01	13,91	16,35	15,05
(d) Education ...	1,60	1,92	2,08	2,65
(e) Medical ...	1,17	2,13	2,68	3,20
(f) Other heads ...	98	2,63	3,01	2,82
3. Pensions and miscellaneous civil charges.	1,35	2,41	2,59	3,31
4. Civil Public Works ...	6,40	17,47	18,81	24,85
5. Other charges and adjustments.	7,01	4,81	3,84	4,53
Total Expenditure ...	44,48	66,48	71,91	81,61
Closing balance ...	9,28	10,44	4,53	27,50

TABLE IX.

Income and Expenditure of local boards in Assam.

—	Average for 10 years ending 1899-1900.	Years, 1900-01.	Years, 1903-04.
Income from—	Rs.	Rs.	Rs.
Provincial Rates	6,14,598	6,44,921	6,13,555
Civil Works	6,889	1,382	2,583
Pounds	61,459	69,201	75,987
Ferries	1,04,474	1,00,102	1,04,139
Contributions	2,22,323	2,43,299	3,39,118
Other sources	67,846	68,649	1,17,613
Total Income	10,77,589	11,27,554	12,52,995
Expenditure on—			
Refunds	3,974	3,207	2,659
Post Office	41,336	43,065	42,777
General Administration ...	2,784	2,793	2,814
Education	1,86,186	2,15,522	3,28,459
Medical	71,000	97,219	99,578
Civil Works	6,82,681	7,82,248	6,11,433
Other heads	83,705	79,275	1,25,828
Total Expenditure ...	10,71,666	12,23,329	12,13,548

TABLE X.

Income and Expenditure of municipalities in Assam.

—	Average for 10 years ending 1899-1900.	Years.	
		1900-01.	1903-04.
	Rs.	Rs.	Rs.
Taxes on houses and lands	41,915	44,411	56,179
Other taxes	53,366	66,817	66,531
Rents	5,724	7,132	6,155
Grants from Government and Local Boards.	40,031	67,953	69,147
Other sources	56,806	59,575	67,941
Total Income	1,97,842	2,45,888	2,65,953
Expenditure on administration and collection of taxes.	17,240	18,404	18,860
Public safety	6,954	10,400	11,453
Water-supply and drainage—			
(a) Capital	31,548	25,555	19,275
(b) Maintenance ...		19,595	19,293
Conservancy	55,267	76,940	80,713
Hospitals and dispensaries ...	7,198	8,029	8,965
Public Works	46,410	58,293	71,074
Public Instruction	6,060	7,806	8,942
Other heads	23,673	24,527	22,290
Total Expenditure	1,94,850	2,49,549	2,60,865

TABLE XI.

Statistics of the Civil and Military Police Force in Assam.

—	1881.	1891.	1901.	1903.
Civil Police—				
Supervising staff—				
District and Assistant Superintendents.	10	9	16	16
Inspectors	20	20	20	21
Subordinate staff—				
Sub-Inspectors ...	57	59	116	137
Head constables ...	180	256	236	226
Constables	1,259	1,779	2,308	2,289
Union and Municipal Police	111	15	15	15
Rural Police... ...	5,304	6,792	6,854	6,807
Military Police—				
Officers	255	273	354	343
Men	2,086	2,156	2,674	2,527
	Rs.	Rs.	Rs.	Rs.
Expenditure* ...	8,87,067	12,38,449	19,68,849	18,86,252

* Includes figures for rural police.

TABLE XII.

Statistics of the Jails of Assam.

—	1881.	1891.	1901.	1903.
Number of District jails.	4	9	9	7
Number of Subsidiary jails (Lock-ups).	17	13	15	17
Average daily jail population—				
(a) Male ...	1,408	1,577	1,600	1,434
(b) Female ...	53	35	33	25
Total ...	1,461	1,612	1,633	1,459
Rate of jail mortality per 1,000	43	52	25	28
	Rs. a. p.	Rs. a. p.	Rs. a. p.	Rs. a. p.
Expenditure on jail maintenance.	1,20,594 0 0	1,24,513 0 0	2,32,829 0 0	1,80,701 0 0
Cost per prisoner	82 8 8	99 12 9	142 9 2	123 13 9
Profits on jail manufactures.	*45,882 0 0	28,548 0 0	13,357 0 0	9,410 0 0
Earnings per prisoner.	34 0 0	25 15 0	9 3 0	7 6 0

* Chiefly on extra mural labour.

TABLE XIII.

Statistics of Colleges, Schools, and Scholars in Assam.

Institutions.	1890-91.			1900-01.			1903-04.		
	Number of institutions.	Scholars.		Number of institutions.	Scholars.		Number of institutions.	Scholars.	
		Males.	Females.		Males.	Females.		Males.	Females.
Public.									
Arts Colleges ...	...	...	...	1	49	...	2	120	...
Upper secondary schools...	13	3,325	...	23	4,907	...	26	6,116	...
Lower ,, ,,	93	6,991	93	127	8,888	185	122	8,560	382
Upper primary ,, ...	102	} 57,607	4,538	111	4,290	371	94	3,472	257
Lower ,, ,, ...	2,120			2,895	76,263	8,126	2,732	74,298	5,483
Training schools ,, ...	16	290	41	22	350	30	7	373	58
Other special schools ...	7	202	8	17	849	...	22	1,155	...
Private.									
Advanced	96	1,852	...	89	2,427	4	76	2,384	...
Elementary	189	3,919	18	173	3,008	53	151	3,443	179
Total	2,641	74,186	4,698	3,458	101,031	8,769	3,232	99,921	6,359

Akā Hills.—Section of the sub-Himálayan Hills lying north of the Darrang District, Assam, between the Dhansiri and Dikrai rivers. The hills have steep serrated ridges covered with dense forest, but, owing to the inhospitable nature of the country and of its inhabitants, have never been properly explored. The Akā tribe is divided into two sections, nicknamed the Hazári-khoás, or 'tribe supported by a thousand groups of ryots' and the Kapás-chors or 'thieves who lurk in the cotton fields,' and in the time of the Assam Rájás, they regularly harried the inhabitants of the plains. For many years the chief of the Kápás-chor tribe, Tagi Rájá, violated our boundaries, and in 1829 he was captured and lodged in the Gauháti jail. In 1832, he was released but immediately resumed his attacks, and in 1835 massacred all the inhabitants of the police outpost and British village of BALIPARA. Six years later he surrendered, and an agreement was made by which both sections of the tribe received a yearly allowance in consideration of good conduct. In 1883, Medhi, the Kapás-chor chief, detained a mauzadár who had visited his villages, while his brother carried off from Bálipára a clerk and ranger in the employ of the Forest department. A punitive expedition was despatched which occupied Aká territory and recovered the captives, with the exception of the mauzadār, who had died. Since that date they have given little trouble, but in 1900 a party of armed Akās forcibly entered the shop of a trader at Bálipára, in order to exact the amount which they alleged was due to them for rubber tapped in the hills. A fine was imposed on the tribe, but in order to minimise the chances of friction it was decided to discontinue the practice under which coolies had been sent into the hills to tap rubber, and to leave the hillmen to bring down this product themselves. The Akās are apparently of Tibeto-Burman origin, and, though a small tribe, are warlike and independent. Their strength lies in their position which enables them to attack British subjects without difficulty, while punitive expeditions sent into their hills are costly out of all proportion to the damage inflicted on the enemy. An account of the Akās will be found in Colonel Dalton's Ethnology of Bengal.

Daflā Hills.—Section of the Himálayan range lying north of the Darrang and Lakhimpur Districts, Assam, between the Rangānadī on the east and the Bhareli on the west and occupied by the Daflā tribes. These tribes are of Tibeto-Burman origin, and are of short, sturdy physique with a Mongolian type of countenance. They are much less united than the Akās, their neighbours on the west, and are thus less formidable to Government. In the time of the Ahom Rájás the Daflás were accustomed to levy blackmail upon the people of the plains, and this custom was the cause of much trouble till 1852 when they were finally induced to commute their claims for a money payment. In 1872, they raided a village of Daflás in the Darrang District, whom they considered to be responsible for the introduction of an epidemic into the hills, killed two persons and carried off 44 captives. A blockade was instituted, but proved ineffectual, and a military force was sent into the hills in 1874-75 which attained the desired object of liberating the prisoners who survived. Since that date the tribe has given little trouble, and though individuals have occasionally been carried off from the plains, their release has been effected without difficulty.

Miri Hills.—Section of the Himálayan range lying north of the Lakhimpur District, Assam, between the hills occupied by the Gallongs and the Rangānadī, and inhabited by the Mīri tribe. The Mīris are of Tibeto-Burman origin, and have tall, well-developed frames, with pleasant countenances of the Mongolian type. Unlike their neighbours they have never given trouble to the British Government, and large numbers of the tribe have now settled on the Assam plains. A full account of the Mīris will be found in Colonel Dalton's Ethnology of Bengal.

Abor Hills.—Section of the Himālayan range lying on the northern frontier of the Province of Assam, between the Siom river on the west and the Dibáng on the east, occupied by tribes of Tibeto-Burman origin loosely termed "Abors" or "unknown savages." Owing to the difficulty of the country, and the inhospitable character of the inhabitants, these hills have never been properly explored. The ranges, which are of considerable height, are covered with dense forest, and intersected with large rivers which make their way through wild and precipitous gorges into the plains. The Abor tribes fall into two chief sections, the Passi-Meyongs, who occupy the hills bounded on the west by the Miri country and on the east by the Diháng, and the Bor Abors who live between that river and the Dibáng. The Abors are short and sturdy savages with countenances of a marked Mongolian type. They possess a high opinion of their own strength and importance, and the want of population on the north bank of the Brahmaputra between Dibrugarh and Sadiyá is largely due to the dread of their raids. On several occasions Government has found it necessary to send punitive expeditions into their hills to avenge the murders of British subjects. Such expeditions were despatched in 1858 and 1859, and in 1861 when a fresh massacre took place a few miles from Dibrugarh, preparations were made to establish a chain of outposts along the north bank of the Brahmaputra. The Abors appear to have been impressed by these operations, and entered into agreements under which they were to eceive an annual allowance of iron hoes, salt, opium, and other articles, so long as they continued to be of good behaviour. For some years the tribes remained quiet, but in 1889 four Mīris, who were British subjects, were decoyed by Passi-Meyongs across the frontier and killed. The guilty villages were punished by a fine, but in 1893 the hillmen again broke out and cut up a patrol of three military police sepoys. A few weeks later a second attack was made on a police patrol, one of whom was killed and one wounded. An expedition was then sent into Abor territory which occupied the principal villages after meeting with a good deal of resistance, and as a further punishment a blockade was imposed against the tribe, which was only withdrawn in 1900. These measures appear to have made some impression upon the Abors, and their conduct of recent years has been satisfactory. A full account of their manners and customs will be found in Colonel Dalton's Ethnology of Bengal.

Mishmi Hills.—Section of the mountain ranges on the northern frontier of Assam which shut in the eastern end of the valley of the Brahmaputra, between the Dibáng and the Brahmaputra. These hills are occupied by the Mishmi tribe, and have never been properly explored. They consist, as far as is known, of steep ridges covered, as a rule, with tree forest, and some of the peaks are over 15,000 feet in height. Geologically these hills seem to be a continuation of the Burmese axials. The higher ranges are probably composed of gneiss and granite, and there are some reasons for supposing that they may contain deposits of economic value. Limestone boulders are found in the beds of the rivers issuing from them.

The Mishmis are divided into four tribes, the Chulikáttá or crop-haired, the Bebejiya, the Digáru, and the Migu or Midhi. They are a short, sturdy race of the Tibeto-Burman stock, with features of a Mongolian type. They are keen traders and devoted to a pastoral rather than to an agricultural life, cattle and wives being the chief outward sign of wealth. A full account of these tribes will be found in Colonel Dalton's Ethnology of Bengal. The first expedition into the Mishmi country was made in 1827, and further attempts were made in 1836 and 1845, but none of the explorers succeeded in getting more than three quarters of the way to Rimá, the frontier town of Tibet. In 1851 M. Krick, a French missionary, reached that place and returned in safety to Assam, but on his revisiting the country in 1854 he was treacherously murdered by a Mishmi chief. The offender was captured and carried to Dibrugarh where he was duly convicted and hanged; and attempts were again made in 1869 and 1879 to reach the valley of the Zayul, as the eastern arm of the Brahmaputra is called, but they were unsuccessful. In the cold weather of 1885-86, Mr. Needham and Captain Molesworth marched from Sadiyā to Rimā, but were prevented from going beyond that place by the obstructive attitude of the Tibetan authorities. The path followed ran along the north bank of the Brahmaputra, the total distance traversed being 187 miles For the first 46 miles it lies entirely in the plains, and for the portion of the journey elephants can be used for transport. From here to the Tibetan border, 26 miles west of Rimá, travelling is somewhat difficult. The track is rugged and uneven and crosses ranges of hills varying from 1,000 to 3,500 feet in height, but these difficulties disappear on entering the Zayul valley. The upper portion of this valley was described by M. Krick as a tract cultivated as far as the eye could see, and abounding in herds of oxen, asses, horses, and mules, and in groves of bamboo, laurel, orange, citron and peach trees. Pandit A. K. who entered the valley from the east described the winter crops as rice, millets, and pulses, while wheat, barley and mustard ripened in the spring. The Mishmis do a good deal of trade both with the Zayul valley and with Assam. They receive from the Tibetans cattle, woollen coats, swords, metal vessels, and other articles and give them in exchange Mishmi *teeta* (a plant much valued as a febrifuge), musk, and Mishmi poison.

In 1899, the Bebejiya Mishmis murdered three Khamti British subjects and carried off three children. An expedition was despatched against them in the following cold weather, which, after a tedious and difficult march, succeeded in recovering the captives and burning the guilty villages. The Bebejiya country lies to the east of the Dibáng river and was entered by the Maizu pass which is 8,900 feet above sea-level.

Khamti Hills.—Hilly country on the frontier of Assam, lying at the eastern end of the Brahmaputra valley and inhabited by the Khamtis, a tribe of Shan origin, who are said to have migrated northwards to the hills near the upper waters of the Irrawaddy and [illegible]g when Mogaung was taken by Alaung-payā about the middle of the 18th century. A section of the tribe moved on into Assam and settled near Sadiyá, and their leader succeeded in establishing his position as the feudal chief of the surrounding country. He was recognised by the British when they took over the territories of the Ahom prince, but his son declined to abide by the decisions of the local British officer, and was deprived of his office and dignities. The Khamtis then rose, raided the settlement at Sadiyá, and killed the Commanding Officer, Colonel White, in 1839. The rising was, however, quickly suppressed, and no trouble has since been given by the tribe.

Bor Khamti, the principal stronghold of this people, consists of the valley of the Namkiu (the western branch of the Irrawaddy) with the surrounding hills. It can be reached *viá* the PATKAI and the Hukong valley, or by a route running south-east from Sadiyá up the valley of the Diyun, over the Chaukan pass, which is 8,400 feet above the level of the sea. The distance from Sadiyá to Putau, the principal Bor Khamti village, is only 197 miles. After Bishi the path is very difficult in places, and runs through dense forests where there are no villages and no means of obtaining supplies. Oaks, rhododendrons, and beeches grow freely on the hills, and large game, such as elephants and rhinoceros, are common. Putau is situated in a valley, but is shut in on every side except the south by hills, which in the winter are crowned with snow. The valley is about 25 miles long by 15 broad and is about 1,500 feet above sea-level. The villages are surrounded by a palisade about 12 feet high, made of split trees interlaced with bamboo. The houses are large commodious structures built on piles, and the audience chamber in the Rájá's house is some 50 feet in length by 40 wide. Rice is the staple crop grown in the valley, but pulse and poppy are also cultivated, the Khamtis being much addicted to the use of opium. The people are much more civilized than most of the hill tribes on the north-east frontier, and near Putau there is a brick built temple 95 feet high with a gilded cupola. Some of the images of Buddha in this temple are of considerable artistic merit. The Khamtis have been described by Dalton (Ethnology of Bengal). They seem to stand in some awe of the Singphos who adjoin them on the west, and the Khakus, who are said to be of the same race as the Singphos, who occupy the hills on the east. Little is known about the geology of the tract, but pyrite, calcho-pyrite, and galena are found in this locality.

Singpho Hills.—Tract of hilly country lying to the south-east of the Lakhimpur District, Assam, inhabited by the Singphos or Kachins as they are called in Upper Burma. Their original home seems to have been near the sources of the Irrawaddy, but they have gradually moved southwards and have crossed the Hukong valley and the Pátkai and have entered the valley of the Brahmaputra. The Singphos first settled in Assam towards the end of the 18th century, their villages being located on the Buri Dihing and on the Tengapáni east of Sadiyá. By degrees they assumed a state of semi-independence, and offered some resistance to our troops when upper Assam came under British rule. It was then found that their villages were full of Assamese slaves, and no less than 6,000 were released by Captain Neufville, the officer in command. The Singphos live in small villages, several of which usually own a *quasi*-allegiance to one chief. Their houses are raised on piles, and are often 100 feet in length by 20 broad, with an open balcony at the end where the women of the family sit and work. They form a large element in the population of the Hukong valley which lies to the south of the Pátkai range.

Manabum.—Range of hills lying on the extreme eastern frontier of the Lakhimpur District, Assam, between 27° 30′ and 27° 47′ N. and 95° 54′ and 96° 18′ E. These hills are an outlying spur of the mountain country occupied by the Singphos and Khamtis and mark the eastern limit of the effective jurisdiction of the Assam Government.

Daphabum.—Mountain ridge, situated between 27° 28′ and 27° 47′ N. and 96° 14′ and 96° 55′ E. to the east of the Lakhimpur District. The summit of the highest peak is 15,008 feet above sea level.

Patkai.—Range of hills lying to the south of the Lakhimpur District, Assam, between 26° 30′ and 27° 15′ N. and 95° 15′ and 96° 15′ E. The general height of the range is about 4,000 feet, but it contains summits nearly 7,000 feet in height. The hills are composed of upper tertiary rocks and their sides are clothed in dense forest. The pass over the Pátkai is the recognised route between Burma and the Assam Valley, though, as it entails a long march through wild and hilly country, there is little intercourse between the two Provinces. It was by this track that the Ahoms entered the valley of the Brahmaputra in the 13th century, and it was used by the Burmese when they were summoned to Assam at the beginning of the 19th century to assist Chandra Kanta, one of the last of the Ahom Rájás. In 1837, Dr. Griffiths crossed the Pátkai into the Hukong valley, and in 1896 a railway survey party traversed the range. The estimated cost of the construction of a line from Ledo in the Lakhimpur District over the Pátkai and down the Hukong valley to Taungni station in the Mu valley was 383 lakhs of rupees for a total length of 284 miles. The line, if made, would be carried through the summit of the Pátkai in a tunnel 5,000 feet in length and situated 2,750 feet above the level of the sea. The rocks in that neighbourhood consist of an indurated sandstone. The hills are inhabited by Nágā tribes. Those who live on the Hukong side of the watershed are subject to Singpho chiefs. They are armed with daos, muskets, and cross-bows, and their villages are usually well situated for defence. An account of these people is annexed to the report of the railway survey party.

Mikir Hills.—A tract of hilly country in the Nowgong and Sibsāgar Districts, Assam, lying between the Assam Range and the Brahmaputra about 26° 30′ N. and 93° 30′ E., but cut off from the main mountain system by the valleys of the Dhansiri on the east, and of the Kapili and its tributaries on the west. The northern hills are composed of gneissic rocks, which towards the south are overlain by sedimentary strata of tertiary origin. These younger rocks consist of soft yellow sandstones, finely laminated grey clay shales, and nodular earthy limestone. Limestone is found near the

Námbar, Deopáni, Hariáján, and Jamuná rivers, and iron ore is of widespread occurrence, though the hæmatite is seldom sufficiently concentrated to pay for working. Coal of inferior quality is found near the Langlei Hill and the Námbar river. The hills have steep slopes and both they and the intervening valleys are covered with dense jungle. They extend over an area of about 2,000 square miles and average from one to two thousand feet above the sea, though the loftiest summits attain a height of nearly 4,500 feet. The Mikirs, the tribe inhabiting these hills, speak a language which occupies an intermediate position between Bodo or Kachári and the various forms of Nágá speech. In character and habits they differ entirely from the savage hillmen to the south, and are quieter and more timid than any other tribe in Assam. Dalton states* that they were originally driven from the hills of North Cáchár to the Jaintiá Hills, where they are still to be found in considerable numbers, but the majority of the tribe were displeased with the treatment they received and moved to the locality which has since then borne their name. Similar migrations were undertaken by the Lalungs, a kindred neighbouring tribe, who according to their traditions went to the Jaintiá Hills to escape the necessity of providing the Kachári Rájá with a daily ration of six seers of human milk, and left them, because they did not like the matriarchal theory of inheritance there in force. The Mikirs are said to have been compelled to forswear the use of arms by the Ahom Government, and this is offered as an explanation of their present peaceful disposition. They live in small hamlets near the crops of rice, cotton and chillies, which they raise on the hill side. Their houses are large and strongly built, and are raised on platforms above the ground. Rice is their staple food, but they eat fowls and pork and consume large quantities of fermented liquor.

Assam Range.—Range of hills lying between 24° 58′ and 26° 48′ N. and 89° 49′ and 94° 50′ E. which runs almost due east and west between the valleys of the Brahmaputra and Surmá. It consists of the GARO, KHASI AND JAINTIA, NORTH CACHAR and NAGA HILLS, and at its eastern end trends towards the north and is joined by the PATKAI to the Himálayan system, and by the mountains of Manipur to the Arakan Yoma. The general height is from three to six thousand feet, but at Jápvo in the Nágá Hills, a height of nearly 10,000 feet is attained. The Shillong peak (6,450 feet) is the highest point in the Khási Hills. Geologically the range falls into two groups. The Gáro, Khási and Jaintiá Hills and part of North Cáchár are known as the Shillong plateau, and consist for the most part of a great mass of gneiss. The eastern portion is mainly composed of sandstones of tertiary age. Coal is found in the Gáro and Khási Hills, and the hills to the south of LAKHIMPUR,

* Ethnology of Bengal, page 54.

and lime on the face of the Khási Hills overlooking the plains of Sylhet. Through the greater part of their length the hills take the form of sharply serrated ridges covered with dense forest, but the central portion of the Khási Hills is an elevated plateau consisting of rolling downs covered with short grass.

Barail (Big Dyke).—Range of hills in North Cáchár, Assam, lying east and west between 25° 5′ and 25° 20′ N. and 92° 32′ and 93° 29′ E. and connecting the Jaintiá and Nágá Hills. The range, which is for the most part composed of soft greenish sandstone, has sharply serrated ridges, and is covered with dense forest and bamboo jungle. Several of the peaks are nearly 6,000 feet in height. The Jatinga river makes its way through these hills to the Barák, and the Assam-Bengal Railway has been carried up the valley of this river.

Japvo.—Highest mountain in the Province of Assam (9,890 feet) situated in the Assam Range a little to the south of Kohīmá (Nágá Hills District) in 25° 36′ N. and 94° 4′ E.

Nokrek.—Highest peak in the range of hills, on the western slope of which lies Turá, the headquarters station of the Gáro Hills District, Assam. This range rises sharply from the lower hills with which it is surrounded, and the summit and sides are clad in dense tree forest. Nokrek is situated in 25° 27′ N. and 90° 19′ E., and reaches a height of 4,652 feet above the level of the sea.

Tukreswari.—Hill in Habrághát pargana, Goálpára District, Assam, in 26° 3′ N. and 90° 38′ E. on the summit of which was a temple dedicated to Durgā built by a former Rájá of Bijni. Its construction indicated considerable engineering skill on the part of the architect, and it was frequented by pilgrims from all parts of India. The temple was destroyed in the earthquake of 1897, and is now being rebuilt.

Saraspur or Siddheswar Hills.—A range projecting from the Lushai system into the Surmá Valley, Assam. The hills run north and south between 24° 26′ and 24° 52′ N. and 92° 30′ and 92° 35′ E. and form the boundary between Sylhet and Cáchár. The height varies from 600 feet to 2,000 feet above sea-level; the slopes of the hills are steep and covered with tree forest, and are composed of sandstones and shales of tertiary origin.

Bhuban Hills.—A range of hills projecting from the Lushai system into the southern part of the Cáchár District, Assam. The hills lie north and south between 24° 15′ and 24° 45′ N. and 92° 52 and 93° 5′ E. on the eastern border of the District, and form the watershed between the Barak and Sonai rivers. Their height varies from 700 feet to 3,000 feet and their slopes are very precipitous. They are formed of sandstones and shales of tertiary origin, thrown into long folds. A temple sacred to Bhuban Baba, a local name for Siva, stands on the summit of a hill about 30 miles south-east of Silchar. Manipurīs, up-country men, and garden coolies resort to this place on the occasion of the Sivarātri, the Srīpanchami and the Barunisnan, and bathe in a tank in the neighbourhood of the temple, and make offerings at the shrine.

Brahmaputra (Son of Brahmā or God).—A river of Tibet and north-eastern India, which for its size and utility to man ranks among the most important in the world. Its total estimated length is about 1,800 miles, and its drainage area about 361,200 square miles, while during the rains the flood discharge at Goālpāra is said to be more than half a million cubic feet of water per second. An element of romance hangs over the river, as a certain portion of its course has never been actually explored, though there is little doubt that the San-po, or great river of Tibet, pours its waters through the DIHANG into the river which is known as the Brahmaputra in the Assam Valley. The source of the San-po is in 31° 30′ N. and 82° E., near the upper waters of the Indus and the Sutlej, and lies a little to the east of the Mānasarowar lakes. It has been traced almost continuously for a distance of 850 miles eastwards to Gya-la-Sindong, which is barely 150 miles from the Assam frontier, but no explorer has yet succeeded in following the river right down to its junction with the Brahmaputra. It was at one time thought that the San-po might be identical with the great river of Burma, the Irrawaddy, but explorations which terminated in 1882 proved that the course of the San-po could not lie east of a place called Samā in the Zayul valley. It was then suggested that the river that flowed past Samā was not identical with the stream that runs westward from the Brahmakund to Sadiyā, but was a tributary of the San-po, which flowed to the west of Samā into the plains of Burma. This theory was completely disproved by the explorations of Mr. Needham, who in 1885-86 marched from Sadiyā up the so-called Brahmaputra to Rimā, a village east of Samā, and proved that the river at Rimā and the river that flowed past Sadiyā were the same. The San-po having no outlet towards Burma in any direction, there is little room for doubt with regard to its identity with the Brahmaputra. Granted this premise, it seems probable that the channel by which it makes its way through the Himālayas is the Dihāng, which is by far the largest river that falls into the Brahmaputra from the north, and at the point of junction considerably exceeds in volume the river flowing from the east, which, as it follows the same direction as the united stream in its passage down the valley, has been wrongly styled the Brahmaputra by the Assamese. In 1886-87, the San-po was visited by a native explorer, who stated that he followed its course nearly 100 miles south of Gya-la-Sindong to a place called Onlet, which is only 8 miles from Miri Padam and 43 miles from the Assam frontier. At first sight, it may seem strange that a geographical problem of such interest as the identity of the San-po and the Dihang should still remain unsettled, and that such a small strip of territory should be allowed to remain unexplored. The hills through which the Dihāng makes its way present, however, great difficulties to the explorer, and are inhabited by fierce and hostile tribes of whom little is known. Activity in that region is politically undesirable, and even if no opposition was offered to the expedition, it is possible that an advance and subsequent retirement would be construed into a sign of weakness, which might embolden the hill tribes to make incursions on the frontier of Assam. The Dihāng at Pobha joins a river flowing from the east, which is sometimes styled the Brahmaputra, sometimes the Luhit. This river rises to the north-east of the hills inhabited by the Mishmis, and is known at Rimā as the Zayul Chu. Near Sadiyā, shortly above its junction with the Dihāng, it receives the NOA DIHING from the southern, and the DIBANG and Sesseri from the northern bank. The most important tributaries that fall into the river west of the Dihāng are, on the north bank, the SUBANSIRI, BHARELI, DHANSIRI, BARNADI, MANAS, SANKOSH, DHARLA and TISTA; on the south the greater affluents are the BURI DIHING, DISANG, DIKHO, JHANZI, DHANSIRI KULSI and JINJIRAM.

Below Dibrugarh the Brahmaputra at once assumes the characteristics by which it is generally known. It rolls along through the plain with a vast expanse of water, broken by innumerable islands, and exhibiting the operations of alluvion and diluvion on a gigantic scale. It is so heavily freighted with suspended matter that the least impediment in its stream causes a deposit, and may give rise to a wide-spreading almond-shaped sand-bank. On either side, the great river throws out large branches, which rejoin the main channel after a divergence of many miles. One of these divergent channels is the Luhit, which takes off from the main stream, under the name of the Kherkutiā Suti, opposite Buri Dihingmukh. It receives the great volume of the Subansirī, and is then called the Luhit; and thus reinforced, rejoins the main stream, nearly opposite Dhansirimukh. The great island or *char* of the MAJULI, with an area of 485 square miles, is enclosed between it and the main stream. Another large divergent channel is the KALANG, which takes off from the south bank opposite Bishnāth in Darrang District, and traverses the whole of Nowgong District west of that point, rejoining the Brahmaputra a short distance above Gauhāti town.

Unlike many rivers that flow through flat low-lying plains, instead of creeping along in a sluggish channel, the Brahmaputra in the Assam Valley has a comparatively swift current, and possesses no high permanent banks. At certain points in its course it passes between or by rocky eminences, which give a temporary fixity to its channel, as at Bishnāth, Silghāt, Tezpur, Singriparbat, Gauhāti, Hāthimurā, Goālpāra, and Dhubri. Where not so controlled, it sends its shifting channels over a vast extent of country, without forming any single continuous river trough.

After a course of 450 miles south-west down the Assam Valley, the Brahmaputra sweeps southward round the spurs of the Gāro Hills, which form the outwork of the watershed separating the Brahmaputra from the Sylhet river system of the Surmā.

It enters the Rangpur District in 25° 47′ N., and 89° 49′ E., and its southerly course continues thence for about 148 miles, under the name of the JAMUNA, through the open plains of Eastern Bengal, as far as its confluence with the Padmā, or main stream of the GANGES at Goalundo in 23° 51′ N., and 89° 46′ E. The united rivers subsequently join the MEGHNA estuary opposite Chāndpur, in 23° 13′ N., and 90° 33′ E. The main stream of the Brahmaputra formerly flowed south-east across the centre of the Mymensingh District, and, after discharging its silt into the Sylhet swamps, and receiving the SURMA united directly with the Meghnā. This was the course shown on the maps of Rennell's survey of 1785, and it was not till the beginning of the 19th century that, having raised its bed and lost its velocity, the river was no longer able to hold its own against the Meghnā, and, being forced to find another outlet for its banked up waters, suddenly broke westwards and joined the Ganges near Goalundo. The old bed still retains its name, but has been steadily silting up, a process which was expedited by the great earthquake of 1897. The entire lower portion of the Brahmaputra may be described as an elaborate network of interlacing channels, many of which run dry in the cold season, but are filled to overflowing during the annual period of inundation. Numerous islands are formed by the river during its course, most of which are mere sandbanks deposited during one rainy season only to be swept away by the inundation of the following year. The principal tributaries after leaving the Assam Valley are the DHARLA and TISTA on its right bank; the latter joins it a few miles to the south west of Chilmārī in the Rangpur District.

In agricultural and commercial utility, the Brahmaputra ranks next after the Ganges, and with the Indus, among the rivers of India. Unlike these two rivers, however, its waters are not largely utilized for artificial irrigation, nor are they confined within embankments. The natural overflow of the periodic inundation is sufficient to supply a soil which receives, in addition, a heavy rainfall; and this natural overflow is allowed to find its own lines of drainage. The plains of Eastern Bengal, watered by the Brahmaputra, yield abundant crops of rice, jute, and mustard, year after year, without undergoing any visible exhaustion.

The Brahmaputra is navigable by steamers as high up as Dibrugarh, about 800 miles from the sea; and in its lower reaches its broad surface is covered with country craft of all sizes and rigs, down to dugout canoes and timber rafts. It is remarkable that there is comparatively little boat traffic in the Assam Valley itself. Goālpāra is the great emporium of the boat trade, and Gauhāti is ordinarily the extreme point reached by boats of large burthen. Nearly all the boats which resort to Goālpāra and Gauhāti come from Bengal or the United Provinces. Large cargo steamers with their attendant flats and a daily service of smaller and speedier passenger vessels ply on the Brahmaputra between Goalundo and Dibrugarh. The upward journey takes four and a half days to complete, the downward three. The principal places passed in the upward journey on the right bank are Sirājganj, a great emporium for jute and other agricultural produce, Dhubri, Tezpur, and Bishnāth, and on the left bank Goālpāra, Gauhāti, Silghāt, and Dibrugarh. There are, however, 18 other ghāts at which the steamer calls, the most important being Shikārighāt for Golāghāt, Kakilāmukh for Jorhāt, and Disāngmukh for Sibsāgar. The downward traffic chiefly consists of tea, coal, oilseeds, timber, hides, lac, and raw cotton from Assam; and jute, oilseeds, tobacco, rice, and other food grains from Eastern Bengal.

Dibāng.—Large river which rises in the Himālayas and, after flowing through the hills inhabited by the Mishmis, falls into the Brahmaputra near Sadiyā. Its course has never been explored owing to the difficulty of the country and the inhospitable character of the surrounding tribes. Bomjur, the most advanced British outpost on the north-east frontier, is situated on the left bank of the river, near the mouth of the gorge through which it debouches on the plains.

Dihang.—Large river which falls into the Brahmaputra a little to the west of Sadiyā. It flows through the hills inhabited by the Abors, and owing to the difficulty of the country and the savage character of the inhabitants, its course has never been explored. The arguments in favour of the view that the Dihāng is identical with the San-po of Tibet will be found in the article on the BRAHMAPUTRA.

Dihing, Noa.—River which rises in the Singpho Hills, Assam, and flows west and then north, falling into the Brahmaputra east of Sadiyā. Through a large part of its course, it passes through jungle land, though here and there the villages of Phakials Singphos, and Assamese are to be found upon its banks. It is not largely used as a trade route, but a boat of four tons burthen can proceed as far as Singri Samon's village in the dry season and beyond the Inner Line, which marks the effective limits of British jurisdiction, in the rains.

Dibru (or Sonāpur).—A river in the southern half of Lakhimpur District, Assam, which flows from east to west, nearly parallel to the Brahmaputra, for about 100 miles, and finally empties itself into that river just below the town of Dibrugarh, to which it has given its name. Of recent years the erosive action of this river has carried away valuable sites in the Dibrugarh bazar.

Dihing, Buri.—River which rises in the Pātkai range and flows in a westerly direction through the Lakhimpur District, Assam, till it falls into the Brahmaputra, after a course of about 150 miles. Its principal tributaries are—on the right bank the Digboi, the Tipling, the Tingrai, and the Sesā, and on the left bank the Tirāp and the Namsang. After leaving the hills, it flows along the southern border of the District past the important settlement at Mārgheritā. It then winds through an outlying spur of the Assam Range, passes Jaipur, the site of an old cantonment, Nahorkhutiya, where it is crossed by the Assam-Bengal Railway, and Khowāng, and during the last part of its course forms the boundary between the Lakhimpur and Sibsāgar Districts. A boat of four tons burthen can go as far as Jaipur in the dry season, and well above Mārgheritā in the rains. At this time of year small feeder steamers occasionally come up as far as Jaipur to carry away the tea manufactured on the estates which are situated in the neighbourhood. Below Jaipur the floods of the river do some damage, and steps are now being taken to repair an embankment which was constructed in the time of the Ahom Rājās. The spill water is, however, said to have a fertilizing effect, where the flood is not deep enough to injure the crop. The river is crossed by two railway bridges and five ferries, and on the eastern border of the District is connected by a channel with the Noa Dihing.

Disāng.—River which rises in the hills inhabited by independent Nāgā tribes and enters the eastern corner of the Sibsāgar District, Assam. It flows west through that District and falls into the Brahmaputra about eight miles north-west of Sibsāgar town. Its approximate length is 140 miles, and the principal tributaries are, on the right bank, the Dimau and Diroi, and on the left, the Taokāk and the Safrai. A boat of four tons burthen can proceed up the Disāng as far as Dillighāt in the rains, and to Mohmārāghāt in the dry season. Feeder steamers visit the latter place in the rains to carry away tea. In the lower part of its course the Disāng passes through cultivated land and its floods cause considerable damage. An embankment, 19 miles in length, has been constructed along the left bank, but this does not afford sufficient protection, and an extension of the work is under the consideration of Government. The river is spanned by a bridge on the Assam-Bengal Railway near the Nāmrūp station and is crossed by eleven ferries.

Dikho.—River which rises in the hills inhabited by independent Nāgā tribes and falls into the Brahmaputra after flowing north and west through the Sibsāgar District, Assam. Its total length is about 120 miles, and most of its course through the plains lies in well populated country, Sibsāgar and Nāzirā being the chief places on its banks. A boat of four tons burthen can proceed up the river as far as Bihubar in the rains, and Nāzirā, though with some little difficulty, in the cold weather. During the rains a feeder steamer plies between Nāzirā and the Brahmaputra two or three times a week. Prior to the construction of the Assam-Bengal Railway the Dikho was of considerable importance as a trade route, but some of the traffic has been diverted to that line. In the lower part of its course, floods do much damage, and protective embankments are now under construction. The river is spanned by a bridge on the Assam-Bengal Railway at Nāzirā and crossed at eight points in the plains by ferries.

Jhānzi.—River that rises near Mokokchūng in the Nāgā Hills District, Assam, and, after a northerly course through the Sibsāgar District, falls into the Brahmaputra. Its total length is 71 miles and in its course through the plains it forms the boundary between the Sibsāgar and Jorhāt subdivisions. In the dry season it becomes very shallow, but during the rains a boat of four tons burthen can proceed as far as the foot of the hills. Molasses, tobacco, salt, oil and other articles of commerce are brought up the river in the rains and sold or exchanged for betel-nut. Tea used formerly to be sent down stream to Jhānzimukh, but most of it is now exported by rail. An area of about 30 square miles in the Simaluguri mauza is injured by the floods of the river, but there are some compensating advantages, as the silt is said to have a fertilizing effect. The Jhānzi is crossed by a bridge on the Assam-Bengal Railway and by four ferries.

Bhogdai.—River which rises in the Nāgā Hills District, Assam, and falls into the Brahmaputra after a north-westerly course through the Sibsāgar District. In the upper part of its course it is styled the Disai and the name Bhogdai is said to have first come into use at the end of the 18th century, in memory of a feast given to the labourers employed on the deepening of the lower channel. Mariāni, a considerable tea centre, and Jorhāt are situated on the left bank of the river, but there is not enough water in the channel to allow of its being used as a trade route. In the lower part of its course floods do some damage, and small protective works have been constructed. The silt is, however, said to have a very fertilizing effect. The river is spanned both by railway and road bridges at Mariāni and Jorhāt, and is 81 miles in length.

Subansiri.—A great river in the north-east of the Province of Assam, which contributes to form the main stream of the Brahmaputra. Its source has never been explored, but it is supposed to rise far up among the mountains of Tibet, and to flow for a long distance in an easterly direction before it turns south to break through the northern mountain barrier of the Assam Valley. It enters the District of Lakhimpur from the Miri Hills through a gorge of great beauty, and, still flowing south, divides the subdivision of North Lakhimpur into two almost equal portions. Before it reaches the Brahmaputra, it forms, together with the channel of the Luhit, the large island known as the Mājuli *char*, and finally empties itself into the main stream, at the western end of the Sibsāgar District. In the hills the bed of the river is greatly broken up by rocks and rapids; but it is navigable by small steamers in the plains. A boat of four tons burthen can proceed to the frontier of Lakhimpur at all seasons of the year, and small steamers ply twice a week to Badati in the cold weather, and twice a month to Bordeobām in the rains. Tea, rubber, mustard, potatoes, pulse, rice, cane and timber are brought down the river, and gold can be washed from its sands, though all attempts to find the matrix of these deposits has hitherto proved fruitless. The river is too wide to bridge, except at an enormous cost, but it is crossed by eleven ferries.

Luhit.—Name which is sometimes applied to the BRAHMAPUTRA, and more particularly to the channel which separates the Mājuli island from the Lakhimpur District.

Dhansiri.—River which rises in the Nāgā Hills District, Assam, and for a considerable distance forms the boundary between that District and Nowgong. At Dimāpur it enters the Sibsāgar District and flows north-north-east to Golāghāt, where it turns to the west and falls into the Brahmaputra after a total course of 180 miles. The upper portion of the Dhansiri valley is a plain of considerable width, shut in between the Nāgā and the Mikīr Hills, and covered with dense tree forest, and, except in the neighbourhood of Golāghāt, the greater part of the course lies through jungle land. A boat of four tons burthen can proceed as far as Golāghāt in the dry season and Dimāpur in the rains, but, owing to the sparseness of population on its banks, the river, in spite of its size, is not largely used as a trade route. A sma steamer runs from Dhansirimukh to Golāghāt every week in tl rins and collects tea from the gardens in the vicinity. Canoes are floated down the river and cotton is brought down by Nāgās in the cold weather. The Assam-Bengal Railway crosses the Dhansiri at Bokājān, and there are five ferries at different parts on its course.

Bhareli.—A large river which rises in the Himālayas in the territory occupied by the Akā and Daflā tribes and enters the Darrang District, Assam, through a gorge of great beauty. After debouching on the plains it flows in an easterly direction round a range of low hills, and then pursues a tortuous course with a generally southern direction to the Brahmaputra, which it joins about 8 miles above Tezpur, after a total course of 160 miles. This, however, is a new channel and the old course runs from Bamgaon to a point about one mile east of Tezpur. The principal tributaries are, on the right bank, the upper Sonai and the Mansiri, and on the left bank the Diji, the Namiri, the upper, Khari, Bar, and Dikrai. During the rains the Bhareli often overflows its banks, and the result is that the greater part of its course through the plains it flows by tree forest or uncultivated land. There are no places of importance on its banks, and this fact, coupled with the swiftness of the current, renders it of little use as a trade route. A ferry on the trunk road crosses the river which, during the rains, is about 250 yards in width at this point.

Dhansiri.—River which rises in Towang, a province subject to Lhāsa, and enters the Darrang District in Assam a little to the north of Udalguri. From there it flows south-south-east and falls into the Brahmaputra. At the place where the river leaves the hills there is a deep pool called Bhairabkund, which is regarded with veneration by the people in the neighbourhood. In 1902 the river changed its course and entered the bed of the Rowta, and since that date its floods have done some damage in the Orāng mauza. For the greater part of its course it flows through jungle, and the total area of cultivated land affected is comparatively small. The river is not used either for irrigation or as a trade route, and its spill water is supposed to deposit sand, not silt.

Kalang.—An offshoot of the Brahmaputra, which leaves the main stream about ten miles east of Silghāt, and after a tortuous course of about 73 miles through the Nowgong District, rejoins the parent river on the confines of Kāmrūp. In the upper part of its course it receives the rivers which flow from the western watershed of the Mikīr Hills, while the KAPILI, with its affluents the Jamunā and the Doiāng, the Barpāni and the UMIAM, bring to it the drainage of the North Cāchār and the Khāsi and Jaintiā Hills. The Digru, another considerable river, joins it near its western mouth. Through the greater portion of its length the banks of the

Kalang are lined with villages, the most important of which are—Kaliābar, Sāmaguri, Purānigudām, Nowgong, the District head-quarters, and Rahā, but at its western end the country through which it passes lies too low for cultivation, and the banks of the river are covered with dense jungle grass. A sandbank at its eastern end is a serious obstacle to traffic during the dry season, but in the rains a steamer of low draught plies between Nowgong and Silghāt, and carries away the tea collected at various centres. Country boats come up from Gauhāti at all seasons of the year for the transport of mustard, which is grown in large quantities in this portion of the Province. In the dry season the Kalang is fordable at Nowgong and Rahā, but after its junction with the Kapili there is always a considerable depth of water in the channel. Ferries have been established across the river at Kuwarital, Nowgong, Rahā and Jāgi.

Kapili.—River which rises on the northern slopes of the Jaintiā Hills, Assam, and, after a course of 163 miles, falls into the Kalang at Jāgi, near the western end of the Nowgong District. It receives the Doiāng, which carries off the whole of the drainage of the extreme north of the Cāchār District, and, in addition to numerous other minor streams, the Jamunā, the Barpāni, and the Umiām or Kiling. A branch channel connects it with the Kalang at Rahā some twenty miles east of its main junction with that river. In the rainy season the Kapili is navigable by boats of four tons burthen up to Panimur, the place at which it leaves the hills, but progress beyond this spot is checked by a barrier of rocks, over which the river is precipitated in a fine waterfall. During the dry weather a boat of this size cannot proceed further than Kāmpur. In the hills the Kapili flows along a rocky channel; in the plains its course is through lowlying land, and its banks are for the most part covered with dense jungle grass. Most of the hill trade, which consists of cotton, lac, and *eri* silk, comes down the Kapili to Chāparmukh, and is despatched from there by rail or country boat to Gauhāti. The Assam-Bengal Railway crosses the river on a brick bridge 500 yards in length, but this is largely in excess of the actual breadth of the channel at most seasons of the year. The principal places on its banks are Chāparmukh, Jamunāmukh, Khārikhāna, and Dharamtul. The floods of this river do considerable damage. Efforts have been made by the villagers to protect their lands by constructing an embankment about seven miles long along the southern bank from Deonarikoli to Magurgaon in the Sahari mauza.

Umiām.—River which rises in the Khāsi Hills, Assam, a little to the north of Maoflang and flows along a deep and precipitous gorge near the station of Shillong. At Barpāni, it is spanned by a fine iron bridge on the cart road between Shillong and Gauhāti, and from that point it flows north-east towards the Jaintiā Hills For some distance it forms the boundary between the Khāsi and the Jaintiā Hills, and finally falls into the Kapili in the Nowgong District, where it is known as the Kiling river, after a course of 81 miles.

Digru (or Sonāpuriā).—River of Assam, rising in the Khāsi Hills, and flowing north-eastwards into Kāmrūp District, where it emerges near the village of Sonāpur, whence it is sometimes locally known as the Sonāpuriā. It joins the Kalang river just above the junction of the latter with the Brahmaputra after a course of 64 miles. In the Khāsi Hills, the Digru is known as the Um-thru.

Barnadi.—River which rises in the Himālayas and enters the plains of Assam at 26° 13′ N. and 91° 48′ E. From this point it once formed the boundary between the Kāmrūp and Darrang Districts, but the river has so often changed its channel that its present course is no longer recognised as the boundary. Near the hills the Barnadī flows through forest and grass jungle, but further south villages appear on the banks. The most important places are Sonārikhāl, where two small fairs are held, and Magamuri market in the Tāmulpur tahsīl, which is situated about four miles from the Barnadī, but is a considerable centre of river-borne trade. A ferry plies throughout the year at Dumunichaki on the trunk road. The river is largely used as a trade route and boats of four tons burthen can proceed as far as Sonārikhāl throughout the year, and to Malmurāgaon in the rainy season. It has a total length of about 100 miles.

Kulsi.—River which rises in the Khāsi Hills, Assam, a little to the west of Shillong, and flows north and west for 120 miles to the Brahmaputra, which it joins near the western boundary of the Kāmrūp District. The most important places on its banks are the Kulsi plantation and Chaygaon, a market in Kāmrūp. The upper part of its course lies in jungle, but in the central portion of Kāmrūp it passes numerous villages. It affords an outlet to the timber of the Kulsi plantation, and a certain amount of lac and cotton is brought down it from the hills. The trunk road crosses the Kulsi on two iron bridges at Kukurmārā and Chaygaon.

Manas.—River which rises in the Bhutān hills and enters the valley of the Brahmaputra at the point where the Kāmrūp and Goālpāra Districts of Assam meet. It once formed the boundary between these, but its channel is subject to frequent changes, and for the greater part of its present course it flows through Goālpāra. The principal tributaries are—on the right bank the Makra, Dulani, Ai, Pomajan, Bhandura, and Koija, and on the left bank the Chaulkhoā The banks are, as a rule, covered with jungle, and the river is not much used as a trade route above its junction with the Chaulkhoā, though boats of four tons burthen could probably go as far as Mowkhoā at all seasons of the year. Some damage is caused by the floods of an old channel known as the Mora Manās. The total length of the Manās is about 200 miles.

Ai.—River which rises in Bhutān and has a tortuous easterly course through the Goālpāra District, Assam, till it falls into the MANAS. Its principal tributaries are the Buri Ai and the Kānāmukra, both of which join it on the left bank. For the greater part of its course the Ai flows through jungle land, but it is used for the export of rice, mustard, thatching grass and timber, and is one of the routes by which articles of merchandise are conveyed into the interior. A boat of four tons burthen can proceed as far as Koliagaon in the rainy and Chamugaon in the dry season. The river, which is 95 miles in length, is nowhere bridged, but is crossed by ferries in four places.

Champamāti.—River which rises in Bhutān and after a tortuous southerly course through the Goālpāra District, Assam, falls into the Brahmaputra after a course of 125 miles. It is of considerable use as a trade route, timber and rice being exported down its course, while the ordinary stores of the village trader are carried up it into the interior. In the rainy season a boat of four tons burthen can proceed as high as Garubhāsā, but in the dry weather cannot get further than Basugaon. The most important places on its banks are the markets at Garubhāsā and Chāpar Kāzipāra.

Saralbhanga.—River which rises in Bhutān and flows in a tortuous southerly course through Goālpāra District, Assam, till it falls into the Brahmaputra. Its principal tributary is the Gaurāng, which gives its name to the lower reaches of the river. Through the greater part of its course it flows through jungle land, but it is one of the recognised trade routes of the District by which timber and other forest produce are exported. During the rainy season, a boat of four tons burthen can proceed as far as Pātgaon, north of the trunk road. The total length of the Saralbhāngā is about 81 miles.

Sankosh.—Large river which rises in Bhutān, and at the point where it debouches on the plains forms the boundary between the Districts of Goālpāra in Assam and Jalpaigurī in Bengal. It then flows along the western boundary of the Ripu Duār, and at Maktaigaon divides into two branches. The western arm retains the name of the original river, and, after flowing through Jalpaigurī and Cooch Behār rejoins the eastern branch, which is called the Gangādhar, near Pātāmāri. The combined stream is then known as the Dudhkumār and falls into the Brahmaputra below Dhubri. For the greater part of its course it flows through jungle land, but it serves as a trade route, down which timber, thatching grass, and other forest products are brought. The river is nowhere bridged in Goālpāra, but is crossed by ten ferries. The total length is about 200 miles.

Jinjiram.—River which rises in the Urpad *bhil*, Goālpāra, Assam, and flows through the southern portion of the District, till it falls into the Brahmaputra, south of Mānikarchar, after a course of 120 miles. The most important places on its banks are Lakhipur, South Sālmāra, and Singimāri. Above Sālmāra the country is under water during the rains, and a boat of four tons burthen can proceed as far as Lakhipur. In the dry season it cannot get above Singimāri. The river serves as a trade route for the southern portion of Goālpāra and the Gāro Hills.

Surma.—River in Assam which gives its name to the southern of the two valleys which originally constituted that Province. It rises on the southern slopes of the great mountain range which forms the northern boundary of Manipur. From there it flows for about 180 miles in a south-westerly direction till it reaches British territory at Tipaimukh. The upper part of its course, where it is known as the Barāk, lies through narrow valleys shut in on either side by hills that rise steeply from the river, and for a short distance it forms the boundary between the Nāgā Hills and Manipur. At Tipaimukh it turns sharply to the north and for some distance divides Cāchār from Manipur in a line almost parallel to that taken by the river in its downward sweep. Near Lakhipur it turns west and enters the Cāchār District, through which it flows with an extremely tortuous course till Sylhet is reached at Badarpur. A few miles west of that place the river divides into two branches. One stream is known as the Surmā and flows near the foot of the Khāsi and Jaintiā Hills past Sylhet, Chhātak, and Sunāmganj, and then turns again towards the south. The second branch is known at first as the Kusiyārā, but after its confluence with the Manu it again divides into two branches. The northern arm is called the Bibiyānā and afterwards the Kālni and rejoins the Surmā on the borders of the District near Ajmiriganj. The lower branch, which is known as the Barāk, resuming the name by which the river is known in Manipur and Cāchār, passes Nabiganj and Habiganj and falls into the Surmā a little to the west of that place The total length of the Surmā, measured along the northern arm of the river from its source to its confluence with the old stream of the Brahmaputra near Bhairab Bazar, is about 560 miles. The Barāk receives numerous tributaries, the most important being on the north the Jiri, Jatinga, Bogapani and Jadukata, and on the south the Sonai, Dhaleswari, Singla, Langai, Manu, and Khowai. In the upper part of its course it flows in a very deep channel, and though rain in the hills often make the river rise many feet in a few hours, it seldom overflows its banks. Lower down, where the bed of the river is not so deep, its waters sometimes spread over the surrounding country, and the floods both of the Surmā and of the Kusiyārā are said to do some damage. In a low lying District like Sylhet, which receives an enormous rainfall, it is practically impossible to confine rivers within embankments, and the only works of this nature constructed on the Surmā are a small embankment along the north bank of the Kusiyārā from Fenchuganj to Mānikkonā, and a raised road from Noakhali to Sylhet along the south bank of the Surmā. Prior to the construction of the Assam-Bengal Railway, the Surmā, with its numerous branches, was practically the only means of communication between Cāchār and Sylhet and the outside world, and it still takes a large share in the carrying trade of the country. During the rainy season, large steamers proceed up the Kusiyārā to Silchar, while steamers of lighter draught ply between Silchar and Lakhipur, and from Markhali near the western border of Sylhet past Sunāmganj and Chhātak to Sylhet town. In the cold weather the large steamers go to Chhātak, and only small steamers can pass up the Kusiyārā to Silchar, as at that season of the year there is very little water in the river. The surface of all the numerous channels of this river is dotted over with native boats of various shapes and sizes at all seasons of the year, and in that part of its course where it flows through or in the neighbourhood of the hills the scenery is extremely picturesque. Its importance as a trade route has caused many local marts to spring up on its banks. The most important of these are—on the river prior to its bifurcation, where it is known as the Barāk—Lakhipur, Silchar, Siyāltek, and Badarpur, where it is spanned by a magnificent railway bridge. On the Surmā, or northern branch, lie Kānairghāt, Sylhet, Chhātak, Dwārā Bazar, and Sunāmganj; while on the Kusiyārā are found Karīmganj, Fenchuganj, Bāliganj, Manumukh, and Ajmiriganj. These are, however, only the more important centres of local trade. Throughout the whole of its course in the plains the banks of the various branches of the river are lined with villages, and there are numerous markets of less importance.

Jiri.—River which rises on the southern slopes of the Barail, Assam, and, after a southerly course of 75 miles, falls into the Barāk or Surmā. For nearly the whole of its length it forms the boundary between the Cāchār District and Manipur State, and it is crossed at Jirighāt by a ferry, which is maintained for the use of travellers along the Silchar-Manipur road. The greater part of its course lies through hilly country, and there is very little cultivated land in the vicinity. The only traffic brought down by the river consists of forest produce and tea from a garden which is situated at Jirighāt, about five miles above its confluence with the Barāk.

Sonai.—River which rises in the Lushai Hills, Assam, and, after a tortuous northerly course of 60 miles through the Cāchār District falls into the Barāk. As far as Maniārkhāl it flows through jungle land, but in the lower part of its course its banks are fringed with villages. The most important of these are Palanghāt and Sonaimukh. A boat of four tons burthen can proceed as far as Maniārkhāl during the rains, but the river is not largely used as a trade route.

Jatinga.—River which rises near Hāflang in the North Cāchār hills, Assam, and flowing west and south falls into the Barāk. The hill section of the Assam-Bengal Railway has been taken up the valley of the Jātingā, the line running along the right bank of the river. In the plains the Jātingā passes near numerous tea gardens, and during the rainy season a small steamer goes up to Bālāchara near the foot of the hills. The river is nowhere bridged, but is crossed by five ferries, and is largely used as a trade route. Barkhalā Bazar, Bālāchara, and Dāmcharā railway station are the most important places on its banks. Its total length is only 36 miles.

Dhaleswari.—River which rises in the Lushai Hills, Assam, where it is known by the name of Klangdong, and, after flowing north for 180 miles, falls into the Barāk at Siyāltek. Changsil, one of the earliest British outposts in the Lushai Hills, is situated near its right bank, and the river is still used as a trade route as far as Sairang, a few miles from Aijal, the headquarters of the Lushai Hills. At Pollycharā the Dhaleswari enters the Cāchār District, and from this point flows through the fertile Hailākāndi valley. During the rains small feeder steamers proceed up the river as far as Kukicharā twice a week, and in the dry season their place is taken by ordinary country boats. The river passes by numerous tea gardens and bazars, the most important mart being Siyāltek. The banks are steep and high, and the channel deep, but the river is liable to sudden freshets, which occasionally do some damage to villages in the neighbourhood, and small embankments have been erected on two or three gardens to prevent the spill water from injuring the tea. The Dhaleswari used formerly to run along the west side of the valley and fall into the Barāk near Badarpur, but one of the Kachāri Rājās is said to have diverted its course close to Rangpur, and this new channel is known as the Kātākhāl. The old channel is now completely cut off from the upper waters of the Dhaleswari by an embankment, but the bed still contains a good deal of water, and between June and September a boat of four tons burthen can proceed above Hailākāndi as far as Ainākhāl.

Singla.—River which rises in the Lushai Hills, Assam, and flowing northwards through the Karīmganj subdivision of the Sylhet District falls into the Son lake forty-five miles from its source. On emerging from this lake it is known as the Kachuyā, and falls into the Kusiyārā, a branch of the Surmā, a little to the east of Karīmganj town. In the upper portion of its course it flows through jungle land, which is still very sparsely peopled, but about eight miles north of the Sylhet boundary it enters on an elevated tract, which has been planted out with tea, and from there to its junction with the Kusiyārā its banks are fringed with villages and tea gardens. There is very little road traffic in Sylhet, and the Singlā is largely used as a trade route which gives an outlet to tea, forest produce, rice, and other products of the country. During the rains a boat of four tons burthen can proceed as far as Dullabcharā, but even in the dry season traffic is carried on in light vessels, which are towed up stream.

Langai.—River which rises in the hills to the south of the Sylhet District, Assam, and flows north to within a few miles of Karīmganj town. Here it turns to the south-west and finally disappears in the Hākāluki *haor* (depression). During the rainy season it is connected with the Kusiyārā branch of the Surmā river near Karīmganj by a channel called the Natiākhāl. On entering Sylhet, the river flows through a reserved forest, part of which has recently been thrown open to cultivation, and then through low hilly country, planted out with tea, and from this point its banks are fringed with tea gardens and villages. There is little wheeled traffic in Sylhet, and the Langai is largely used as a trade route, which affords an outlet for forest produce, tea, rice, cotton, mustard, mats, and other country products. During the rainy season a boat of four tons burthen can proceed as far as Hāthikirā tea estate: in the cold weather traffic is carried on in light vessels. The most important places on the banks of the Langai are Pāthārkāndi, Nilām Bazar, Lātu, and Jaldhub. Its total length is 78 miles.

Manu.—River which rises in Hill Tippera, and, after flowing in a tortuous north-westerly course through the Sylhet District, Assam, falls into the Kusiyārā branch of the Surmā a little to the east of Bahādurpur. Almost the whole of its course in the plains lies through cultivated land and it is largely used as a trade route, for the carriage of forest produce of all kinds, tea, rice, and oil-seeds. A boat of four tons burthen can proceed as far as the frontier of Hill Tippera in the rainy season, but during the dry weather traffic is carried on in vessels of lighter draught. The river passes a large number of local centres of trade, the most important of which are Lalbāg and Maulavi Bazar. A little to the east of the latter place it receives a considerable tributary in the shape of the Dholai. The total length of the river is 135 miles.

Khowai.—River which rises in Hill Tippera, and, after flowing north-west through the Habiganj subdivision of the Sylhet District, Assam, falls into the Barāk near Habiganj. The river passes by numerous local centres of trade, the most important of which are Muchikāndi and Habiganj, and is largely used as a trade route. During the rains a boat of four tons burthen can proceed as far as Bāllā Bazar in Hill Tippera, and even in the dry weather a vessel half that size can nearly reach the frontier of the District. The total length of the river is 84 miles.

Bogapani.—River which rises on the east of the Shillong peak in the Khāsi Hills, Assam, and after flowing west and south through the hills past Maoflang and Shellā falls into the Surmā at Chhātak. In the lower part of its course it is an important trade route and affords an outlet to limestone, oranges, bay leaves and other products of the hills. The total length of the Bogāpāni is 52 miles.

Jadukata.—River which rises in the Khāsi Hills, Assam, where it is known as the Kynchiang or Panātīrtha and, after flowing west and south debouches on the plains of Sylhet. Here it divides into two main channels, that to the east being known as the Pātlai and further on as the Bolai, that to the west as the Piyain. Both of these branches fall into the Kanksa, and the united stream ultimately joins the Surmā in the Mymensingh District a little to the west of Habiganj. The river is largely used as a trade route, and affords an outlet to the products of the Khāsi Hills. During the rainy season it is often unable to carry off the enormous quantities of water precipitated in its catchment area, and considerable damage is then done by floods. The total length of the river is 120 miles.

Someswari.—River in the Gāro Hills, Assam. It rises to the north of Turā station, and flows east as far as Darangiri. Here it turns south and debouches on the plains of Mymensingh, through which it makes its way to the Kāngsa river, 88 miles from its source. It is navigable up stream as high as Siju, where further progress is barred by rapids. Valuable outcrops of coal and lime have been discovered in the Someswari valley, but owing to difficulties of transport, they still remain unworked. In its course through the hills, the river flows through gorges of great natural beauty, where precipitous cliffs are smothered with dense tropical vegetation.

Majuli.—Island lying between 26° 45′ and 27° 12′ N. and 93° 39′ and 94° 35′ E. in the north of the Sibsāgar District, Assam, formed by the diversion of the Kherkutiā channel from the main stream of the Brahmaputra. This channel subsequently receives the waters of the Subansirī, in itself a large river, and is then known as the Luhit to the point where it rejoins the parent stream opposite the mouth of the Dhansiri. The island has an area of 485 square miles, a population (1901) of 35,000 souls, and is the site of the AUNIATI, DAKHINPAT, GARAMUR, and other *sattras*, or priestly colleges, which are held in great reverence by the Assamese. The Mājuli is much exposed to flood and diluvion, and the staple crops are summer rice and mustard. It contains numerous streams, lakes, and patches of tree forest covered with beautiful cane brake, and the general effect is very picturesque. The island has but one road and no towns, and an old-world air pervades the place which savours more of the 18th than the 20th century.

Loktak.—Lake situated in the south of the Manipur State in 24° 27′ and 24° 34′ N. and 93° 47′ and 93° 52′ E. It now covers about 27 square miles, but is said to be gradually decreasing in size. The surface is dotted with floating islands of aquatic plants, forming a refuge for fish and wild fowl, which are found there in large quantities. At the southern end, where a range of low hills runs into the lake, there are rocky islands, the sites of fishing villages.

Laur.—Name of Hindu kingdom, which at one time occupied the north-western portion of what is now the District of Sylhet, Assam. Gor or Sylhet proper was conquered by the Muhammadans in 1384 A.D., but Laur retained its independence for another two hundred years. One of the Rājās, named Gobind, was summoned to Delhi and there embraced the Muhammadan faith, and his grandson Abid Reza abandoned Laur and built the town of BANIYACHUNG at the beginning of the 18th century. Under the Mughal empire the Rājās of Laur were held responsible for the defence of the frontier, and their estates were not actually assessed to revenue till the middle of the 18th century. In 1765, Laur came under the civil administration of the British.

Cross-references (for Imperial Gazetteer only).

Barāk.—River in Assam.—*See* SURMA.
Barel.—Hill range in Cāchār District, Assam.—*See* BARAIL.
Bhairabi.—River in Darrang District, Assam.—*See* BHARELI.
Bhimsenā.—River in Sylhet District, Assam.—*See* SURMA.
Bibiyānā.—River in Sylhet District, Assam.—*See* SURMA.
Bogra.—River in Khāsi and Jaintiā Hills District, Assam.—*See* BOGAPANI.
Buri Dihing.—River in Lakhimpur District.—*See* DIHING, BURI.
Dafābhum.—Mountains in Lakhimpur District.—*See* DAPHABUM.
Daphlā.—Hills on the Darrang-Lakhimpur frontier.—*See* DAFLA HILLS.
Dhaneswari.—Rivers in Darrang and Sibsāgar Districts.—*See* DHANSIRI.
Dikhu.—River in Sibsāgar District.—*See* DIKHO.
Disai.—River in Sibsāgar District.—*See* BHOGDAI.
Disoi.—River in Sibsāgar District.—*See* BHOGDAI.
Dudhkumār.—River in Goālpāra District—*See* SANKOSH.
Dufflā.—Hills on the Darrang-Lakhimpur frontier.—*See* DAFLA HILLS.
Gangādhar.—River in Goālpāra District.—*See* SANKOSH.
Jānji.—River in Sibsāgar District.—*See* JHANZI.
Jhiri.—River between Manipur State and Cāchār District.—*See* JIRI.
Kālni.—River.—*See* SURMA.
Kātākhāl.—River in Cāchār District.—*See* DHALESWARI.
Kawahi.—River in Sylhet District.—*See* KHOWAI.
Kiling.—River in Khāsi and Jaintiā Hills District.—*See* UMIAM.
Klangdong.—Upper reaches of the DHALESWARI.
Kopili.—River in Nowgong District.—*See* KAPILI.
Kusiyārā.—River.—*See* SURMA.
Kynchiang.—River in Khāsi and Jaintiā Hills District.—*See* JADUKATA.
Lohit.—River.—*See* LUHIT.
New Dihing.—River in Lakhimpur District.—*See* DIHING, NOA.
Noa Dihing.—River in Lakhimpur District.—*See* DIHING, NOA.
Old Dihing.—River in Lakhimpur District.—*See* DIHING, BURI.
Panātirtha.—Upper course of the JADUKATA.
Somoswari.—River in Gāro Hills.—*See* SOMESWARI.
Sarispur.—Hill range in Cāchār District.—*See* SARASPUR.
Siddheswar.—Hills in Cāchār District.—*See* SARASPUR.
Sonāpurā.—River in Lakhimpur District.—*See* DIBRU.
Sonāpuriā.—River in Khāsi and Jaintiā Hills District.—*See* DIGRU.
Thaleswari.—Place of pilgrimage in Goālpāra District.—*See* TUKRESWARI.
Umthru.—River in Khāsi and Jaintiā Hills.—*See* DIGRU.